The Woodworking, V..... Joinery and Woodturning Starter Handbook

Beginner Friendly 3 in 1 Guide with Process, Tips Techniques and Starter Projects

(3 Manuscripts in 1)

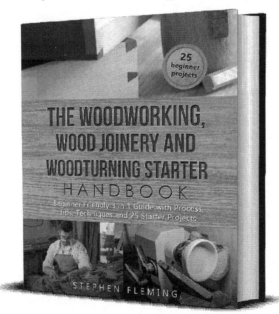

Stephen Fleming

1

Table of Contents

Woodworking for Beginners Handbook

The Step-by-Step Guide with Tools, Techniques, Tips and Starter Projects

Stephen Fleming

Bonus Booklet

Thanks for purchasing the book. In addition to the content, we are also providing an additional booklet consisting of Monthly planner and Project Schedule template for your first project.

It contains valuable information about woodworking and leather craft.

Download the booklet by typing the below link.

http://bit.ly/leatherbonus

Cheers!

Table of Contents

PREFACE

When I first started woodcraft, I was desperately looking for a go-to guide about the processes and tools I would need.

The content I found online was total information overload and wasn't presented sequentially. The books I looked at were either focused on just a few processes or assumed that I already had the necessary information. A lot of the books were also very dated.

There are two ways of learning; one is learning from SMEs (Subject Matter Experts) with years of experience, and the other is people who are just a few steps ahead of you in their journey.

I fall into the latter group. I'm five years into this hobby and still learning from the experts.

I still remember the initial doubts I had and the tips that helped me.

This book is for those who are still running their first lap (0-3 years) in the wood-crafting and want to have a holistic idea of the processes and tools they need.

I have included photographs of realistic beginner projects, and I will explain the process and standard operating procedures associated with them.

In the last chapter, Appendix, I have provided a glossary of woodworking terms, as well as a list of online resources available for free patterns, tips, and techniques.

Cheers, and let's start the journey.

Stephen Fleming

1. Introduction to Woodworking

Tips for Beginners

Tips for Getting Started

- Create a simple woodworking setup to begin with
- Make sure you understand how to take tape measurements
- Make sure you understand basic lumber measurements and types
- Only use straight wood boards to begin with
- Start with just the essential tools
- Sand, sand and sand your wood some more!
- Find out the wood's moisture content before starting work
- Keep your workshop clean and well-lit
- Keep your tools sharp

Safety Tips

- Always remember that the safe way is the right way
- Find out how to safely operate tools before using them
- Make sure all safety equipment is working before starting
- Ensure that the tool's exhaust system is working correctly
- Do not reach through any moving machine components
- Don't talk to others while operating tools
- Do not force anything into the machine
- Turn the tool off before removing blockages
- After switching off the power, do not attempt to stop blades or edges from moving with a stick or your hand
- Know where all emergency switches are
- Do not play with tools or equipment, they are not toys
- Use approved eye protection
- Get first aid for any cut or scratch, no matter how minor

What Is Woodworking? Definitions

So, let's look into various definitions of Woodworking and try to figure out the scope of the craft and the differences between similar sounding terminologies.

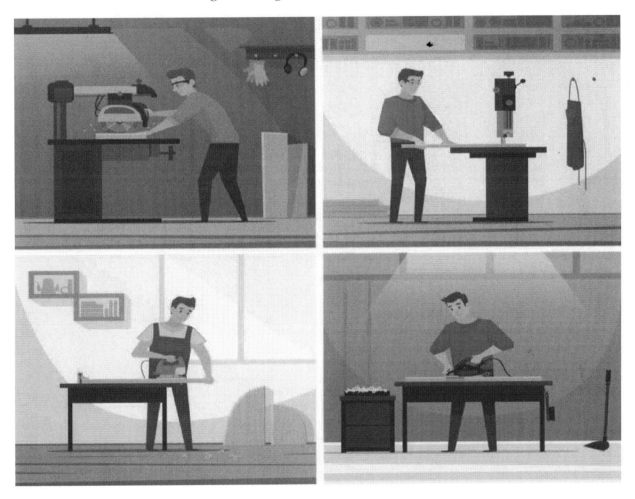

Wood Working

<u>As per Wikipedia:</u>

Woodworking is the activity or skill of making items from wood and includes cabinet making (cabinetry and furniture), wood carving, joinery, carpentry, and woodturning.

So, from the above definition, we can see that woodworking consists of:

-   Cabinet Making

- Wood Carving
- Joinery
- Carpentry
- Woodturning

Let's discuss each of these terms in detail to understand the various subgenres of woodworking.

1. Cabinet Making: This is the art of making wooden cabinets through woodworking skills and tools.

Who is a cabinetmaker?

Someone who builds cabinets for various purposes, as per their customer's specifications, is a cabinetmaker.

Before becoming industrialized, cabinetmakers were accountable for the entire production process of a piece of furniture, from its preliminary conception to its final shape and color.

Carpenter vs. Cabinetmaker

While both professions involve wood, it is the cabinetmaker that goes one step further by concentrating on the finer details of the wood.

It is this attention to detail that distinguishes them from carpenters. Carpenters concentrate on more substantial tasks, such as building large frames, constructing a deck, etc. Cabinetmakers focus on more specific jobs, which are more complicated, like the construction of furniture pieces and cabinets.

Cabinetmakers use a wide range of tools, including a saw table, drum sander, and dust extraction system.

They also carry with them a selection of hand tools like laminate leaners, cordless drills, surface staplers, and jigsaws. They also deal with timber adhesive, nails, screws, dowels, and various other bolts.

2. Wood Carving: This is a form of woodworking that involves sculpting figurines or decorative wooden pieces by carving the wood with a chisel and a mallet.

There are various ways to do wood carving. A few of them are :

- **Whittling:** This is possibly the oldest style of woodcarving, and is done with just a carving knife and a piece of wood. When the sculpting is finished, you can see each 'knife stroke' rather than a smooth or sanded surface. Some carvers, although they primarily use a blade for whittling, will also use a V-tool. A whittling knife may have a "fixed handle" or be a "folding Swiss army knife" style. You can refer to my book: *Whittling for Beginners Handbook: Starter Guide with Easy Projects, Step by Step Instructions, and Frequently Asked Questions (FAQs)* for a detailed discussion on this art.

- **Carving-In-The-Round:** This is a form of carving that typically produces pieces with a much more 'life-like' surface and appearance. A Carving-In-The-Round can take any form. It might be huge or

11

tiny; it could be to scale or have life-like dimensions and also may be repainted, tarnished, or left natural. Carving-In-The-Round and relief carving use a knife, chisels, gouges, etc.

- **Relief Carving:** Relief carvings have a flat back, and are also carved in three dimensions. This design is typically used in displays. However, carvings can be of any subject and are often placed on walls.

- **Chip Carving:** With this type of carving, chip knives are used to chip off the wood. This chipping is done at two levels -the surface and the point beneath where the cut meets. Patterns can be very loose and free or based on geometric shapes such as triangles, circles, lines, etc.
This skill particularly requires a lot of practice.

Whittling   In-The-Round-Carving

Relief Carving   Chip Carving

3. Joinery: Joinery is the technique through which two or more pieces of timber are attached. Joinery can entail the simple gluing, nailing, or screwing of two or more pieces of wood, or it can be far more complex, involving elaborate joints. The primary purpose of joinery is to hold timber firmly together. Joinery is a vital part of the majority of Woodworking and is found in furnishings, cabinets, windows and doors, floor coverings, and many more.

Examples of Joinery

Carpenter at Work

4. Carpentry: If you look into the definitions of carpentry mentioned at various sources like Wikipedia, you will read that carpentry is related to cutting, shaping, and installing wood frames/structures in building, bridges, ships, etc. So, it is associated with the wooden frames used in the construction industry today. Webster's Dictionary describes it as the art of shaping and assembling **structural woodwork.**

5. Woodturning: In woodturning, an item of wood is placed onto a lathe, which rotates the wood quickly. As it spins, the woodworker uses tools such as cuts and blades to delicately cut away at the turning wood to shape it as well as form a pattern of grooves. It's reasonably easy for newbie's to get going and produce easy products, while advanced woodworkers can create more detailed pieces.

Woodturning is typically utilized for items like chair and table legs. These long, thin pieces of wood are suitable for turning, and also make outstanding tasks for beginners. However, woodturning can be used for a lot more tasks, including bowls, vases, candleholders, birdhouses, and more.

Woodturning

Types of Woodworking

You might have an image in your mind of what woodworking entails, but there are various means by which people approach this craft.

Woodworking by hand device

Woodworking with a hand device has had a massive resurgence in the last two decades. Hand-device woodworkers make use of traditional tools and methods to construct points. Hand saws, blades, scrapes, and planes are used, rather than anything that plugs into a wall.

Starting this craft is very economical, yet as your skills improve and you settle into the art form, you will certainly discover that a $200 precision hand plane is pretty useful.

Woodworkers using hand tools most likely feel even more of a connection to the process than any other type of woodworker. It takes patience and has a much longer learning timeline. Also, it's a slower method to master and a whole lot quieter. However, individual satisfaction can be enormous.

Woodworking with Power Tools

I would certainly think that majority of woodworkers today are power-device woodworkers. Woodworker training courses are also geared towards these kinds of devices.

Power devices such as miter saws, table saws, drills, and sanders are ubiquitous and can also be a very budget-friendly method to start building tasks right now.

The biggest downside to using power devices is that they have the potential to cause significant injuries. This shouldn't stop you from using them; however, you need to be aware of safety and how to use them correctly.

Woodworking by Digital Tool

Digital machines have been around for some time; however, they have become extra economical in the past few years and are attracting an increasing number of hobbyists. The main device here is the CNC machine, which makes precision cuts on level items of timber utilizing a router. You will need to format and design all of your work with a computer as well, and the maker will take care of the rest, removing all your items.

The second device some enthusiasts invest in is a laser cutter or engraver. This tool enables you to make even more exact cuts than a CNC, as well as produce some beautiful art.

The most significant downside to using electronic machines is their cost. You can quickly end up spending thousands of dollars. They have their limitations as well, as you will probably still want a table saw and various other power devices. Some individuals feel that digital tools give them less of a "connection" to their woodworking, as well as eliminate the fulfillment of making points by hand.

Special Woodworking

There are two kinds of woodworking for individuals with a real creative streak: woodturning and scrolling.

Woodturning entails using a turret to develop bowls, pins, and various other rounded projects. It's like shaping clay on a potter's wheel, only with wood and blades. The only actual downside to getting involved in woodturning is that lathes can be quite pricey.

Scrolling involves a scroll saw, which is capable of cutting tiny curves and intricate patterns. It takes practice to develop the skill, but you really can develop some spectacular art with a scroll saw. Unlike a turret, scroll saws are relatively economical. They are pretty quiet and don't make a massive mess.

You can indeed find uses for both tools in a standard woodworking store. Perhaps you want to make table legs or add some attractive scrollwork to a fancy cabinet. In general, however, they aren't tools that you will use that often.

Woodworking: Present Scenario

Earlier, we covered the common types of woodworkers.

Many woodworkers are stereotyped as irritable teachers who preside over uninteresting courses to teenage students who don't want to be there, or as the retired grandpa type that putters about in his garage and makes the occasional birdhouse.

Thankfully, those stereotypes are no longer valid. There is even more variety in woodworking now than ever before, thanks to online communities/groups, as well as the lower cost and availability of tools.

In the past ten years, there has been a massive surge in two groups of individuals making woodworking a pastime. Not so long ago, a woman woodworker was an extremely uncommon sight. Today, lady woodworkers are commonplace. There is absolutely nothing about woodworking that anyone can't do.

The second massive demographic spike has been among millennials, individuals in their 20s, as well as 30s. These are the people who are the new professionals or who want to take up a hobby that can help them unwind and relax while making something with their hands.

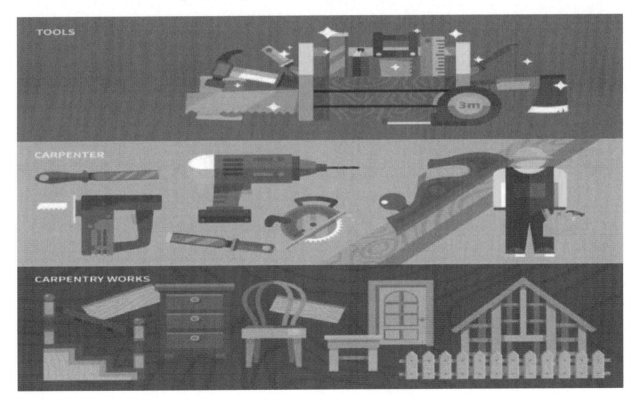

2. About Wood

As a beginner woodworker, the first decision you need to make is the type of wood you want to use for a particular project. There are a lot of options, and it can be very confusing. I'll start with the basics.

For the sake of simplicity, I'll limit my discussion to the most typical products you will come across in woodworking:

- Hardwoods
- Softwoods
- Plywood
- MDF

Understanding wood only comes after years of work, but still, the below discussion will help you at least somewhat in your initial projects.

Solid Lumber

In some cases, the term "lumber" refers merely to solid wood. The wood is milled from a tree, in contrast to made items and sheet items, such as plywood or MDF.

There are two kinds of solid wood to choose from, softwoods and hardwoods. Technically, hardwood is predominantly wood that originates from a deciduous tree that has leaves, like oak or maple.

Also, hardwoods are generally more challenging physically than softwoods. An amusing exemption would be Balsa, extraordinary softwood; however, because the Balsa tree is deciduous, it's considered a hardwood.

Softwood is lumber that originates from the conifer tree, which has needles as well as cones, like an evergreen. Yet typically, when a lot of us discuss hardwoods, we are describing its physical solidity. When I discuss softwoods, I am usually talking about pine.

Expansion & Contraction of Wood

Wood may expand or contract based on the season. Throughout cold or damp months, boards will draw in moisture, causing them to widen. In drier months, they will contract as they shed that moisture. Growth and tightening are vital to understanding when building with solid wood. For small projects, this wood movement is not much of a problem; however, if you are working on a large project such as a tabletop, it will matter.

Softwood

When you go to a residential facility or lumberyard, the chances are that fragrance you detect is pine.

Green Pine

This is one of the most common woods you can purchase and is also typically the most budget-friendly. Pine

20

boards are used in house construction and framework. They are perfect for tasks that you plan to paint; however, a lot of people like the unpainted natural appearance too.

#	Hardwood	Softwood
durability	Highly durable and lasts for several decades	Less durable
color	Darkly colored wood	Usually lightly colored wood
weight	Heavyweight with a rough texture	Lightweight with a fine texture
fiber	Fibers are close and dense	Less fiber
source	Hardwood is collected from deciduous trees	Softwood is collected from evergreen trees

Hardwood

When you think about fine furnishings and traditional woodworking, you may imagine wood varieties such as mahogany, walnut, or cherry. Primarily, people buy hardwoods and unique types due to their grain pattern, color, or longevity.

If you want to develop something that lasts hundreds of years, hardwood is an excellent option. Hardwood is rarely tarnished as well, as this would be a waste of money to cover it up with paint. It is usually shielded with a clear overcoat, such as varnish, lacquer, or oil.

Softwood   Hardwood

Hardwoods are excellent for integrating different styles by utilizing different wood. Walnut and maple, for instance, are commonly seen in chess boards.

The thickness of hardwoods can make them tough on devices, and they can be challenging to shape. Less-than-sharp table saw blades are notorious for leaving shed marks on cherry and maple, calling for a great deal of sanding.

The biggest disadvantage is that hardwoods can be costly – particularly more unique types. It may be challenging even to find hardwood lumber where you live. Fortunately, there are online hardwood sellers that will certainly pick out the best boards to ship to you.

One of the most common hardwoods, which is also pretty affordable in the US, is oak. It, together with maple and walnut, are typically available at most relevant stores. Oak has its issues, but it looks good and is a terrific starter choice.

Plywood

Plywood is among the most popular, as well as the most versatile, building materials you can use. It can be one of the most confusing, as there are so many grades with their coded designations.

You can do a Google search for Plywood Grades to read more on this subject. Plywood varies because it is made artificially. Thin veneers of genuine wood are piled in contrary grain and glued together. This crisscrossing is what gives plywood its stamina as well as security.

As a whole, the more layers, the higher the quality. Plywood that comes fine sanded on both sides is best, and also seek out plywood with the least amount of spaces along the edge.

You can also purchase specialized maple, oak, cherry, or other hardwood plywood. These are often on the pricier side.

For store projects, jigs or fixtures, there's absolutely nothing wrong with saving money by purchasing a lesser quality of plywood. It's mostly visual difference.

Less expensive plywood is rough and has knots, but it can be useful for a lot of jobs that don't need a pretty end product, such as shop tasks.

Why use plywood?

There are a lot of advantages to plywood against solid lumber. Firstly, it's reasonably affordable. Also, plywood is very strong and steady: you do not need to stress over-expansion as well as tightening. It won't warp. It's a fantastic option for large surfaces, such as a tabletop.

Drawbacks of Plywood

There are a couple of negative aspects of using plywood. For one, a 4'x 8'ssheet of plywood is heavy and difficult to move and manage alone. Nevertheless, many home centers can cut it down into smaller pieces for you. Steering a complete sheet of plywood can be a challenge.

Second, while the face of the plywood looks excellent, the edges can be an eyesore. You can cover these up with iron-on edge banding or make your very own side banding out of solid timber. If you are feeling a little edgy, though, just welcome the split appearance and use it as a layout element!

A great trick is to run some concealing tape along your cut line when reducing against the grain. Also, make use of a sharp blade. We are using concealing tape to prevent chip-out when crossing the grain on plywood.

MDF

Lastly, I want to speak briefly about Medium Density Fiberboard, or MDF, which is made by pressing wood fibers into boards.

It's not to everyone's taste, but it is economical and can also be really valuable in some tasks. MDF is commonly used in knockdown furniture, like what you may need to assemble from Ikea or other stores. It's typically laminated or coated.

The material itself is easy to work with, as it cuts like butter. It's an excellent choice for small or ornamental indoor projects that you will paint. Also, you do not need to stress over splintering.

Drawbacks of MDF

MDF can be a little fragile, particularly near the edges where it can collapse like cardboard if you aren't cautious. The faces are really strong. If you use it for racks longer than 2 feet or so, they will ultimately sag. It's likewise incredibly heavy: a full-size sheet is not easy to move on your own.

MDF can be vulnerable around the edges. This split can be stopped by simply drilling a hole initially.

However, the most significant disadvantage to MDF is the fine dirt it produces when you sand it. It's certainly not something you want to breathe: wear a respirator and also have a dust collection mechanism connected to your tools.

For starters, you can use free wood. Craigslist is a fantastic source for individuals giving away free lumber. Likewise, if you don't mind a little additional work, think about getting wood from old pallets. I've broken down plenty of free oak pallets. Above all, have fun, and don't hesitate to try something brand new!

3. Woodworking Tools

Introduction to Basic Tools

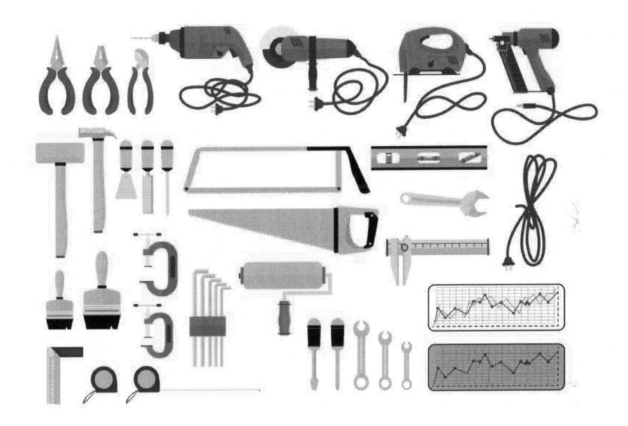

List of Essential Tools for a Beginner:

Basic Hand Tools

- **Workbench:** A wooden workbench is the pivotal tool of a woodworker's workshop. If you're really on a tight budget, using clamps to secure your work surface is an excellent replacement for a variety of other tools.

  I would recommend that you either construct a wooden workbench or purchase one if you don't feel capable. Whichever you choose, you need a robust wooden workbench with at least three durable tops, stable, helpful base legs, and at least one strong vice.

Workbench

- **Jack Plane& Block Plane**:

   A jackplane is an intermediate-sized "bench plane." If you're on a tight budget; a jackplane can momentarily be used instead of various other planes that have more specialized functions:
   - rough supply removal
   - jointing board sides
   - smoothing the boards

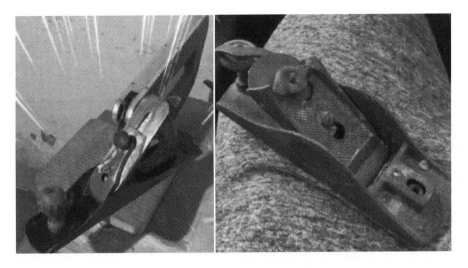

Jack Plane   Block Plane

Block Plane: These little planes can be used to trim your joints, put chamfers on edges, trim end grain, etc. I would recommend a low-angle block plane, as the reduced angle allows you to cut difficult grain much more quickly.

- **Rabbet Plane:** Rabbets are among one of the most common joints in furniture production, so a hand plane that cuts a rabbet must be at the top of your purchase list. Yes, rabbets can be cut without a hand plane. However, it's more challenging.

- **Coping Saw:** This cost-effective tool is used regularly for rough cutting shapes in the board, and particularly for removing waste from dovetail joints (among one of the most common wooden joints). A cost-effective coping saw will work fine, along with a pack of budget-friendly extra blades.

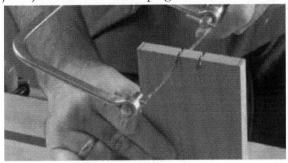

Coping Saw   Hand Saw

- **Panel Saw**: Handsaws (usually called "panel saws") are long, thin saws with a comfortable wooden handle. They are utilized for the harsh dimensioning of your lumber. Although a "panel saw" is technically a smaller handsaw that fits into the panel of a device chest, from this point, I'll refer to this type of saw as a "panel saw" to separate it from the broad classification of "hand saws." Panel saws can be found with two tooth setups: "rip" and "cross-cut." You will certainly need both.

- **Miter Box and Saw**: An excellent miter box & miter saw (a very large backsaw) will allow for cutting the exact right length at the right angles. They will save you a great deal of time when attempting to square your board finishes. The lengthy miter saw glides through a rigid saw frame.

Miter Saw   Marking Knife

- **Marking Knife:** This is used for marking where you will be cutting with your saw or chisel. For challenging situations (like dovetails) and for making very straight lines (which is crucial for tight-fitting joints), you need the perfect marking knife.

- **Chisel:** A chisel is one of the most common tools you will come across. A premium-quality collection of bevel side bench chisels (new or vintage) will last you several years (maybe even your whole life) as well as be useful in virtually every project. I've made use of some affordable plastic grip bench chisels, although I do favor lighter wooden handle chisels with exceptional steel.

Chisel   Tape Measure

- **Tape Measure/Folding Rule**: A "folding rule"(not "ruler") comes before a tape measure and enables you to measure dimensions when cutting boards, etc. If you are on a limited budget, a little tape measure can be used again and again.

- **Rule Guide:** A metal rule is excellent for measuring, but it can be tough to use for a design job. The trouble is the density of the rule itself. It creates a "step" between the surface area as well as the work piece, which can make moving a mark less than accurate. You can use a tiny timber block that makes it easier to accurately mark a line, in this case. You just align the end of the block with the preferred increment on the rule. After that, note the line, utilizing the block as a rule guide.

- **Marking gauge:** This is used for transferring a dimension and duplicating it over. A locking mechanism stops the gauge from slipping, and you from loosing that measurement. You can't effectively create furniture without an efficient and sturdy marking gauge.

Marking Gauge

- **Combination Square, Try Square, and Sliding Bevel Square:** Combination Square is great, as well as accurate, 6-inch mix square, and is used for a lot of jobs in my workshop. Jobs such as inspecting the squareness of boards (when planning them to the last dimension), scribing dovetail joints, gauging the depth of mortises, and much more.

- **Try Square:** This is used to make up work pieces for precise-fitting joints. If you're not confident about constructing your very own try square yet, you need to purchase good steel, try Square. It'll be used for making square lines around the faces as well as sides of the boards, like a line for where to cut with your saw.

29

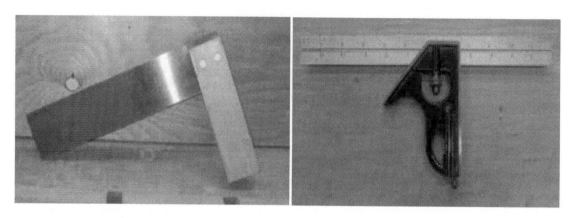

Try Square   Combination Square

Sliding Bevel Square: This is used to scribe angles on your work piece. A good sliding bevel square should have the ability to duplicate an angle repeatedly, like when you are laying out dovetails on a board face.

Sliding Bevel Square

Essential Power Tools

Below are the necessary power tools for a beginner to start their projects.

Table Saw   Compound Meter Saw   Router

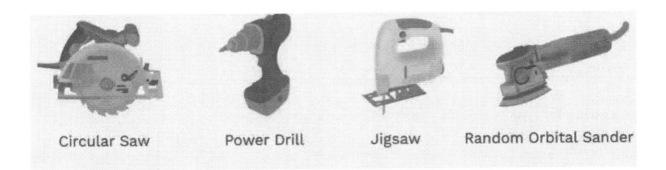

Circular Saw   Power Drill   Jigsaw   Random Orbital Sander

- **Table Saw:** A table saw is a circular saw placed under a table surface area, with a part of the blade extending through the table, where it is exposed and able to cut wood.

- **Miter Saw:** This saw is used to quickly cut crown molding, door structures, window cases, and image frames. Miter saws can also make straight cuts for general do-it-yourself woodworking jobs. You have many options with this type of saw.

Kinds of Compound Miter Saws

Compound Miter Saws - These saws will reduce at a variety of angles but also tilt in one direction (left) to reduce a bevel. This is useful for when you want to cut at two different angles, such as when mounting crown molding.

Dual-bevel Substance Miter Saws - These tilts both left and right, so you can reduce bevels and any kind of angle without having to flip your work piece.

Moving Compound Miter Saws – These saws can slide forward and back, and so are useful for larger pieces of wood.

- **Router**: Wood routers are mobile power devices that are used in practically every woodworking task. The most basic use of a wood router is cutting holes in wood or "routing out" to hollow out an opening in an item of wood, metal, or plastic while still generating finished edges, cutaways, rounded contours and also precisely measured holes.

Different router bits are used for different cuts, as shown below:

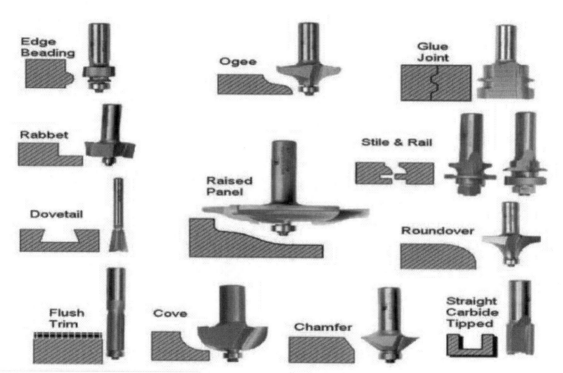

- **Circular Saw:** Some consider this to be more of a carpentry tool than a woodworking one. When a clamp-on straightedge is used, the circular/round saw can be as accurate as a table saw and also handle many of the same tasks, consisting of cutting sheet items such as plywood or medium-density fiberboard (MDF). When woodworking on a budget, a top-quality round saw must be the first portable power device bought.

- **Power Drill:** This is an electrical motor that rotates a replaceable drill bit to make holes in wood.

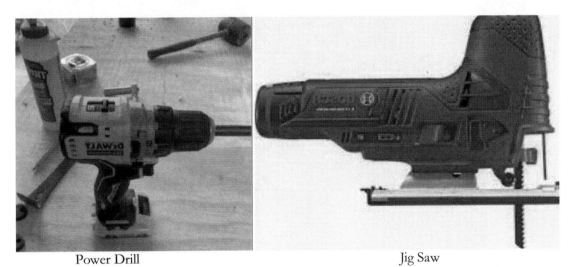

Power Drill   Jig Saw

- **Jig Saw:** The name 'jigsaw' comes from the fact that this saw can cut jigsaw-shaped puzzle pieces. It is a power tool used for cutting curvy lines in timber or other materials. While most saws can just cut in a straight line, a jigsaw makes it less complicated to cut intricate patterns.

- **Orbital Sander:** This is an extremely flexible device for getting a smooth and scratch-free finish, whether Woodworking, plastic working, or metalworking.

;.

Sander

4. Woodworking Process & Techniques

Woodworking Skill Sets for Beginners

- **Learn the different characteristics of timber:** You need to learn whatever you can about various types of wood that you can use for furniture. Features such as firmness, color, density, uses, fractures, the fluctuation due to moisture content, and grain patterns.
- **Knowledge of tools:** You will certainly need to learn how to use different woodworking devices for milling, sanding, boring, carving, and finishing, among others. This includes machine tools like the lathe as well as scroll-saw.
- **Choosing the right screws:** Picking the correct dimension, size, scale, and type of screw is essential in woodworking. While short screws will fail to hold boards together, bigger ones will puncture through the wood.
- **Understanding hand devices:** You will use hand tools like hand planes, blades, clubs, hammers, knives, scrapers, and vises, to name a few. You need to be able to recognize how to use and store these tools correctly
- **Understand various cuts and joints:** Woodworking includes producing multiple cuts and joints, including dovetail joint, mortise, tenon joint, finger joint, biscuit joint, and rabbet joint, among others.
- **Learn about the materials used for finishing:** No woodworking task is complete without a final surface. There needs to be clarity on different kinds of finishing materials like varnishes, discolorations, lacquers, and glosses.

Woodworking Process

1. Cutting the wood down

The first step in the woodworking process is cutting the wood. You will need devices such as the band saw, table saw, and density planer, to name a few, during this stage.

Keep these things in mind while cutting the lumber.

- The cut should be tangential to the annual rings and parallel to the medullary rays to obtain stronger pieces.
- Avoid wasting valuable timber while cutting and leave some room for shrinking, settling, and planning.
- You can cut the lumber with average, quarter, tangential, or radial sawing methods.

Remember that cutting lumber requires a lot of skill and practice. Try to practice as much as you can.

2. Molding

The cut timber needs to be shaped to continue with the project. The mold and mildews you wish to use will depend on the specific job.

So, if you are making a door, for example, you will certainly require the following moldings.

- Astragal-- This is a strip of a semicircular cross-section.
- Bolection-- This is an ornamental molding over or around a panel of the door.
- The case-- This is the frame around the sides of a door.
- Drip Cap-- This is an L-shaped blinking positioned over the door structure to stop water from getting into the door framework.
- Panel-- This has a flat back and raised face, often with elaborate makings. It goes between the stiles and rails that comprise the outdoor frame of a door.
- Stiles and Rails-- Stiles are vertical components, and rails are horizontal and fit around a door panel.
- Structure-- You will need various mold and mildews like head, legs or jambs, a sill or limit, as well as door quit to make up the framework.

Ensure that you prepare a listing of molds you will certainly require to create your furniture piece before starting.

3. Sanding

The next thing to do is sanding. Sanding will help you get rid of mill marks resulting from using various woodworking devices and makers. It can also aid you in eliminating dents or determines, and give you a great finish.

You can use sandpaper with the ideal grit that fits the surface area of the wood. You can generally get woodworking sandpapers that can be found in 80, 100, 120, 150, 180, and 220 grit.

- Generally, 80-100 grit sandpaper is enough to eliminate mill marks and deep scrapes.
- If you are going to stain a piece of wood, use 150-grit sandpaper
- 220-grit sandpaper is best for a surface finish without discoloration.

Conversely, you can use a random-orbit sander for quick and regular sanding, specifically for larger pieces of timber. Make sure to move the sander in the direction of the grain.

You can't use random-orbit sanders for sanding edges or tiny crevices or intricate carvings. The sandpaper is best for this.

4. Staining and dyeing

Both of these techniques boost the visual appeal of the wood. However, they produce varying effects.

- **Staining**

Timber stains comprise a pigment, a service provider, and a binder—the pigment lodges right into the surface area pores of the timber. While the provider helps the pigment to reach the pore, the binder helps them to follow the wood surface area.

Stains are generally extra resilient, particularly oil-based discolorations, and require much less maintenance. Nevertheless, they require a longer dry time, which results in a much better coating. Discoloration can highlight the grain pattern in ash as well as oak.

- **Coloring**

A timber dye normally consists of a colorant and solvent. Unlike a discolor, a dye can penetrate deep into the wood and dim its grain. As a result, the process of dyeing adds dynamic and deep color to the wood.

Dense or figured items of wood are extra suited for the process of coloring, as timber dyes are more translucent. Nevertheless, wood dyes often tend to fade in the sunshine. So, they can't secure the surface of the timber.

5. Constructing

When you have finished dyeing or tarnishing each part, you have to assemble it. At this phase, you will require different fastening products and tools, together with adhesive to get the pieces together.

- Before gluing or attaching two items, dry-fit them first. This will help you make sure the two items fit effectively.
- Make use of the ideal sticky or adhesive for joining different parts of the woodwork.
- Utilize the appropriate clamps to fasten the pieces while the adhesive is wet.
- Glue and assemble the components in stages. Plan the complete set-up.

6. Finishing

After setting up all the parts for your woodworking project, the last step is to add a final surface. The purpose of a timber finish is to protect your furniture from dampness, swelling, cracking, discoloration, etc.

You can look for the following kinds of timber surfaces.

- Oil-Based-- You can use oil surfaces like teak oil and linseed oil to add sparkle to your woodwork. These surfaces do not offer much protection, however.
- Water-Based-- Less harmful, non-flammable, water-based surfaces create a clear covering. Apply them gently as they may swell wood fibers in some cases.
- Varnishes—There are two types of varnish: conversion varnish and polyurethane varnish. Conversion varnish is durable and provides a sturdy glossy surface. But you will require specialized

tools and skills to use it.

- Polyurethane Varnish-- Although this uses a clear coating, several layers can lead to a plastic surface. Polyurethane varnish calls for a 30-day healing period. It is quite durable.

- Wax-- This is easy to use. Although the surface gets a nice luster, a wax surface has very little defense.

- Shellac-- A quick-drying surface area coating, shellac provides a clear or yellowish color coating. It offers moderate defense against water and alcohol.

- Nitrocellulose Lacquer-- This is durable and offers excellent protection. It does have toxic elements, however. You have to use a safety mask to avoid breathing in any harmful fumes.

Woodworking Steps

- **Read the plans.**

Acquaint yourself with plans and procedures before you purchase or cut any timber. Make sure the task is something you can manage.

- **Inspect your products list.**

Organize your checklist to make sure that you can efficiently obtain the products you need.

- **Plan your cut checklist.**

Check all your wood and set out where each cut will go. Select the most suitable part of the board for each part of your project. As an example, pick matching tabletop items for grain patterns and also shade uniformity. Also, plan your cuts to ensure that you do the minimum saw adjustments (do all the crosscuts first and after that all the rip cuts, for instance).

- **Pre-mill all the boards to obtain straight and level pieces**

This works together with the cut list planning procedure mentioned above.

- **Mill the boards to their final dimensions.**

This involves planning and jointing the boards.

- **Cut the joints.**

- **Dry fit the settings to make sure that everything fits effectively.**

Ensure that your settings and subassemblies mesh effectively before you add any adhesive/glue. You should also practice the assembly procedure. Repeat the process until you can do it efficiently.

- **Glue the assembly and clamp it too.**

Work swiftly and pull each joint fully together before proceeding. This reduces the possibility of joint freeze-up. When clamping, beware not to apply to excessive pressure. Use just enough force to draw the joints together. You don't want to squeeze all the adhesive out.

- **Square the components.**

Tabletops must be perfectly level, and various other assemblies should be flawlessly square. Make use of a straightedge to check for monotony and a tape measure (measuring diagonally across the assembly) to help.

- **Clean up.**

Put the assembly aside in a place where it won't get damaged and tidy up.

- **Relax.**

Type of Cuts

When choosing what kind of wood flooring to purchase, many individuals don't consider the cut of the timber—the majority think only about what type of wood they want. But apart from the kind of wood, the kind of cut on the wood is also essential.

There are four cuts of timber that have their own distinctive look: Live Sawn, Plain Sawn, Quarter Sawn, and Rift Sawn.

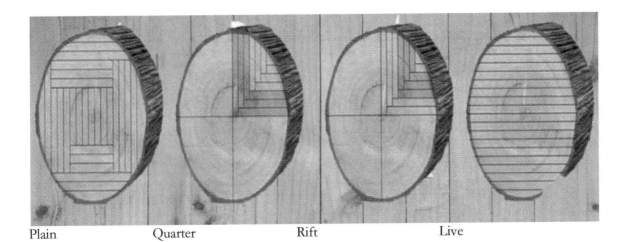

Plain   Quarter   Rift   Live

Live Sawn

39

This cut of wood is one of the most common and inexpensive, and also creates the least quantity of waste when cutting into slabs. Each slab is cut right off the log without moving the alignment.

This cut is best suited for those that desire a more rustic appearance.

Plain Sawn

This cut of timber is also standard and is differentiated by its sawing technique. The board is cut, moved 90 degrees, then cut once more. This cut additionally generates a minimal quantity of waste and produces a cathedral grain pattern

Quarter Sawn

This cut of wood is identified by its grain pattern that runs vertically and has a striped appearance. Planks are cut by dividing the log into quarters; after that, live sawing the timber.

This cut is more expensive due to the production process as well as the lower return of wood per slab.

Rift Sawn

This cut of timber is the most expensive, as well as the least common. The slabs are reduced perpendicular to the tree's development rings. This cut can provide a more modern-day straight grain pattern and is prominent with oak and maple varieties. However, it is challenging to get these kinds of slabs wider than four inches throughout.

Making Straight Cuts

Among the first activity, any woodworker is going to perform is making cuts either by hand or with a power tool.

It may look simple; however, there's some finesse in exactly how to make your cuts precise, square, and as tidy as possible.

Before we begin cutting timber to the required size, let's find an essential aspect of wood dimensions.

Nominal vs. Actual Dimensions

The timber dimensions detailed on lumber are not always the same. It's no secret, as every carpenter recognizes this, yet it's something you need to know before you end up purchasing the wrong size for a task. We've all seen lumber measurements in the shops, like 3x5's, which is showing the cross-section measurement of the lumber - in this example, 3" by 5".

Nevertheless, if you take a tape measure to the wood, you'll notice that it's not truly 3" by 5", it's about a 1/2" shorter on both dimensions, providing you with 2- 1/2" by 4- 1/2".

Part of the reason is that when a tree is felled and chopped up into boards, it has a great deal of wetness/moisture still inside when the wood is kiln-dried, and it diminishes as well as deforms after shedding the wetness.

To make up for this, the mills smooth down the surface areas as well as clean up the sides, ideally offering you a straight as well as smooth board, at the expense of some lumber dimension.

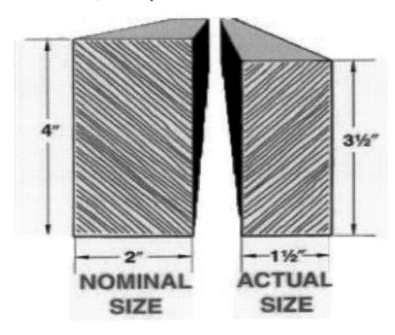

1x4	$\frac{3}{4}"$ x $3\frac{1}{2}"$
1x6	$\frac{3}{4}"$ x $5\frac{1}{2}"$
1x8	$\frac{3}{4}"$ x $7\frac{1}{4}"$
2x2	$1\frac{1}{2}"$ x $1\frac{1}{2}"$
2x4	$1\frac{1}{2}"$ x $3\frac{1}{2}"$
2x6	$1\frac{1}{2}"$ x $5\frac{1}{2}"$
2x8	$1\frac{1}{2}"$ x $7\frac{1}{4}"$
4x4	$3\frac{1}{2}"$ x $3\frac{1}{2}"$
6x6	$5\frac{1}{2}"$ x $5\frac{1}{2}"$

Nominal vs. Actual – Sample Chart

This is correct for great deals of dimensioned lumber, so always check the measurements at the store before purchase.

Understanding this will help you prepare for your tasks and know the real dimensions you require, as well as what you should be shopping for when you pick up lumber.

Kerf

Let's start with the basic definition of kerf from the dictionary:

A slit made by cutting with a saw.

When you are cutting, you usually want to cut on one side of your marking line, so the kerf does not cut into your piece.

Saw kerf

With a circular saw, there's a tiny indent on the home plate; this indent represents the blade kerf. Finding out what the kerf is will help us be more accurate in our design and process. Your saw noting will likely be different! The type of blade you're using could have different kerf too. Always check on your blade configuration.

Layout and Cutting

Cutting wood is very easy; however, it takes a little ability to ensure that the cuts are square, straight, and neat.

To cut a square, we will need to make a square noting. Straighten the edge of your Square along the side of the wood where you wish to cut, and also draw the line with a pencil.

Revolve the Square and make similar lines alongside your cut line, these side cuts will undoubtedly help your blade follow the line.

You can start by measuring the density of the timber; after that, measure the same distance back from the end. Finish by scribing a pencil line around the post with the square side. It may look straightforward, but when your whole project falls apart by 1/8," it can be extremely frustrating.

Plunge Cut

The circular saw is the most popular tool among homeowners, as well as DIY-ers for a few reasons. It is relatively inexpensive, mobile, and simple to manage. It is perfect for cutting timber, especially for making straight cuts in wood.

Can you use your circular saw to cut various shapes in timber? The method for doing this is called a "plunge cut."You can use a plunge cut for many DIY jobs.

A plunge cut is where a cut begins in the middle of the board. Plunge cuts can be a little tricky, but get far easier with practice.

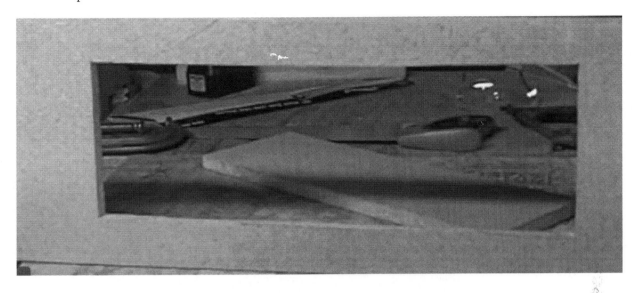

Joints

Below are the significant types of wood joints we use to make wooden furniture or to use in other crafts.

Biscuit Joint

Definition: An oval-shaped piece of typically pressed timber glued right into two crescent-shaped openings.

Use: To join big timber boards together, such as in tabletops.

Box Joint

Definition: An edge joint with interlocking square fingers. A practical option to sync joints.

Use: Making edges of boxes or box-like frameworks.

Bridle Joint

Definition: An edge joint comparable to amortize and tenon, where the through mortise is open on one side and also takes a fork form.

Usage: This joint is used for joining the tops of rafters.

Butt Joint

Definition: The end of one piece of wood is butted with adhesives, nails, screws, etc.

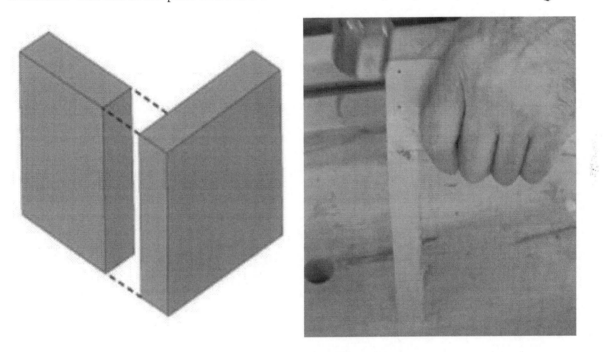

Butt Joint: Can be nailed after gluing

Use: Wall framing on building and construction sites.

Dado/ Housing Joint

Definition: A trench cut across the timber in which another piece is inserted.

Use: Plywood racks and cabinetry.

Dovetail Joint

Definition: A box joint with diagonal interlacing fingers.

Use: Cabinets and boxes.

Dowel Joint

49

Definition: Round small-diameter wood pins placed and glued into the reds of two wood items.

Use: Furniture building and construction.

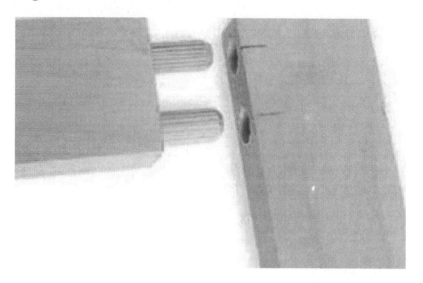

Half Lap Joint

Definition: Two items are cut to half of their thickness and glued together.

Use: Frames for images, boundary door frames, and dirt divider panels for cabinets.

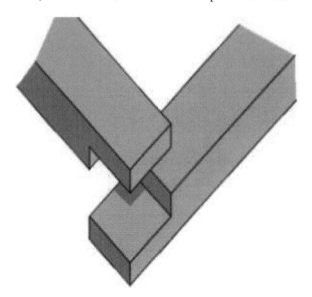

Miter/ Mitered Butt Joint

Definition: A butt joint in which two boards are joined at a 45-degree angle.

Use: Boxes, frames, and light furniture.

Mortise and tenon

Definition: A joint where the tenon (stub) from one piece of wood fits into the mortise (cavity) of another at a 90-degree angle and is finally reinforced with glue.

Mortise

Tenon

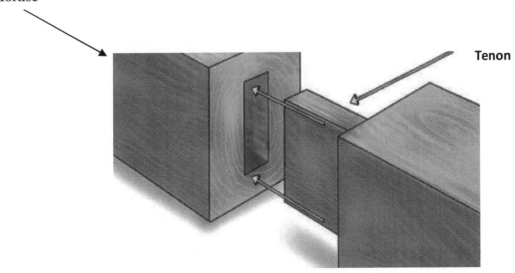

Use: Furniture, like tables and work desks and also building and construction.

Pocket Joint

Definition: This involves joining two pieces through a pre-drilled hole (drilled at an angle) and a screw.

Use: Kitchen cabinetry as well as furnishings.

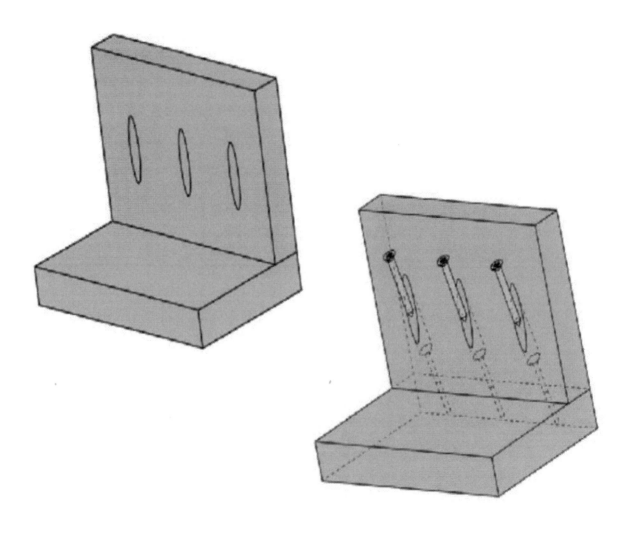

Rabbet Joint

Definition: A type of butt joint with a groove cut into the edge of a piece of wood for a better grasp.

Use: Cupboards and glass panes.

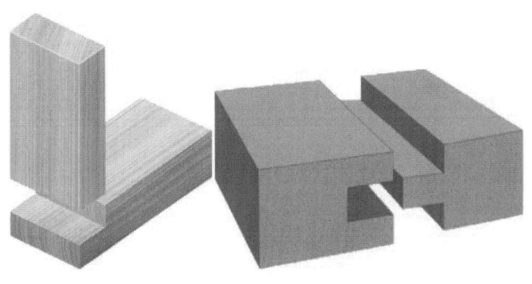

Rabbet Joint   Tongue and Groove Joint

Tongue and Groove Joint

Definition: A protruding groove cut into the length of one wooden piece that fits into the gap of another.

Use Floor covering, parquetry, paneling, and similar building and construction.

5. Safety: Best Practices

Beginners' Safety Tips

1. Always put on safety gear

This may seem obvious, but it needs to be said. When using loud devices like routers and surface planers, putting on ear protection is a must. Similarly, use latex gloves while doing finishes. Always wear your work goggles. These should be the first thing you grab.

Eye Wear

PPE - Personal Protective Equipment

Eye protection is a must! The smallest speck in your eye, regardless of severity, can take you out for the remainder of the day.

Hearing protection, either over-ear or in-ear, provides relief with any power tools. Hearing loss is measured by the period of exposure, so while it might not seem so bad at the moment, by the end of the day, your hearing will have suffered damage.

Dust masks are fantastic for avoiding the inhalation of wood dust. It might appear benign; however, timber dust is listed as a risk by safety organizations.

54

Handwear/Gloves may appear to be missing from this list; however, that's deliberate. While handwear covers are wonderful for many other uses, dealing with woodworking devices is not one of them. If your handwear cover gets stuck while running a woodworking tool, it could pull your hand in with it.

Apart from PPE, other best safety practices are:
- Tying back long hair
- Removing jewelry
- Tucking in loose apparel
- Removing watches

2. Wear the right clothes

The trouble with baggy or loose garments is the risk of them getting caught in a saw blade. So, wear more well-fitted clothing. Also, remove jewelry and watches, especially anything that dangles.

3. Avoid things that adversely affect your reaction time

It's like when you're driving a vehicle: you want to avoid alcohol, drugs, and medication to prevent crashes. Never work while intoxicated. Stay safe!

4. Disconnect the power

Remember to always detach the power source itself prior to altering the blades orbits on your power tools. Along with ensuring the button is off, see to it that there is no power flowing to the tool.

5. Use a single expansion cable

Making use of one sturdy extension cable for all your power devices will ensure that you turn off the power for all at once. Too many cables are confusing and a tripping risk.

6. Never ever use blunt blades &bits

Blunt tools are more dangerous to use, and also make the task far more difficult in general. A well-sharpened tool will make a cleaner cut.

7. Inspect supply for existing steel

Prior to sawing or making a cut, make sure that the item does not have existing nails, screws, or various other pieces of steel lodged into it already. Spinning blades, as well as nails (and various other items of steel), don't mix and will trigger damages to both the stock and the cutting head. It can also trigger stock to fall apart and cause injury, so always make sure (or utilize a steel detector to guarantee for you) that stock is tidy.

8. Work against the cutter

A lot of power devices are constructed in a manner whereby the piece of wood moves via the tool in the opposite direction. So you need to make sure that the blade or router bit cuts against the motion of the wood, as opposed to with it.

9. Never reach over a running blade

Always wait until a rotating blade has stopped moving before reaching over to get rid of waste or cut-offs and so on. To be on the safe side, remove waste by using a push stick or scrap item.

10. Reduce interruptions

When handling interruptions, you should make sure that you finish what you were doing (finishing a cut, specifically when dealing with a power tool) before turning your attention to other places.

Additional Safety Instructions for Woodworkers

Accident or mishap prevention in woodworking essentially starts from the ground up-- the flooring. Below are the factors which help us to attain a safe woodworking workspace.

Clean Workplace

Whether you're cutting, drilling, shaping, or sanding, the process is safer in a clean, minimalist workplace.

Remove sawdust, wood shavings, and chips, as well as junk lumber from the work area throughout the day, to get rid of sliding and stumbling risks.

Immediately clean up oil and other fluids on the floor. Also, be careful of lumber that is sticking out or poorly piled.

The flooring itself also can end up being unsafe. Loose boards, protruding nails, splinters, holes, or other surface issues can cause significant injuries if left unfixed.

Fire Safety

The wood used as a primary material and byproducts like sawdust and shavings are the leading causes of fire. Keep button enclosures, bearings, and motors clean as well as free of sawdust—store oily rags in a steel container with a tight cover.

All store workers must know where to find and how to use firefighting tools in their workplace. The appropriate fire extinguishers should be in place in all locations. If workers use fire extinguishers, companies must provide training once a year.

Handling Small Tools

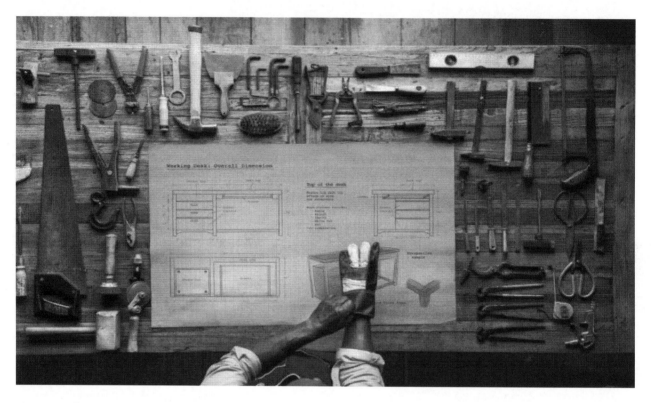

Keep small tools, such as hammers, chisels, punches, or drills, safely stored. Tools left on devices, for example, might cause foot injuries.

Never carry sharp tools in your pockets or use tools with burred or mushroomed heads. Keep an eye out for loose handles and repair them regularly.

When dealing with small devices, follow these tips:

- Select the ideal tool for the task. Makeshift tools are always dangerous to use.
- Sharp devices in good condition are safer
- Hand tools to colleagues by the handle
- Bring only as many tools as you can safely use
- While carrying sharp tools, keep the sharp edges down and do not put them your pocket

Using Electrical Devices

Don't allow the tool to run while you're away. Unmonitored machinery is dangerous. The safe worker makes sure the machinery is entirely shut down, not just turned off, before leaving it, because an unsuspecting employee unfamiliar with the machinery may touch the rotating cutting edge.

All woodworking equipment must have a magnetic start and stop button. This type of control button will not allow the machine to start again after the power supply has been disrupted instantly.

Never clean, oil, adjust or attempt to repair machinery while it is still running. Always shut off the power first.

When cleaning machinery, use a brush to remove sawdust. Make sure to wear goggles.

Routine inspections protect against failures. Both supervisors and staff members should regularly inspect all woodworking machinery, as well as their safety features.

Proactive identification of developing problems allows prompt adjustment and results in a much safer workshop. Always evaluate ground connections on all mobile and stationary electrical equipment.

Protective clothes and equipment

A woodworker with protective equipment

Put on well-fitting clothes to prevent clothing from getting caught in moving machinery components.

Loose coats are especially dangerous. We recommend short-sleeved t-shirts or sleeves rolled up above the elbows. Tie strings on shop aprons in the back.

Do not wear neckties or torn apparel.

Do not wear jewelry such as rings, watches, necklaces, and so on, in the woodworking area.

Bear in mind that there are numerous, ergonomically designed devices.

Safety shoes with metatarsal guards or plastic footwear guards will reduce foot injuries in lumber-handling operations.

Due to dust hazards or flying chips, wear safety glasses with side shields when operating cutting equipment. For grinding as well as cutting operations, use authorized plastic face shields or safety glasses.

Handling the Saw Blade

- **Handling Circular Saws**: Accidents are caused when contact is made with the rotating blade. Training, as well as using appropriate guards, will reduce these risks.

- Preventing kickbacks: The danger of material being thrown by the saw blade is lowered by using a correctly mounted spreader and an anti-kickback gadget. Make sure that your body is out of the line of fire when the wood is being cut.
- Always keep your hands away from saw blade: Use a stick and not your hand to push the wood through.
- Store the blade so that there is no danger of accidental contact.
- Before sharpening the blade, always check it for cracks.
- **Radial Arm Saw:** Radial arm saws are handy — they can be customized for many jobs. However, these adjustments create additional hazards that must be avoided. You must never break this rule: No adjusting the blade while it is switched on.

Handling Jointer and Planar

Jointer vs. Planar first- The jointer is used to flatten one face and Square up to one edge, and the planer is then used to make the second face flat and parallel to the first.

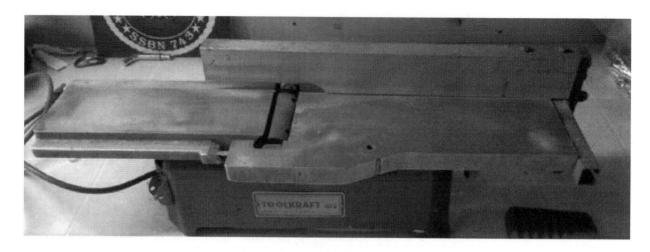

Jointer

Why do we not use the jointer to do the same to other faces and use a planar instead?

It's because the jointer cannot replicate the same flatness on the other face, and the thickness of the wooden plank is not the same throughout. That work can be done by a planar.

Planar

Here are safe practices for:

- **Jointer**

Use jointers only on narrower wooden planks

When doing surfacing work on a jointer, keep both hands on top of the stock

Keep hands off the front or back edge. This is because of the kickback risk as well as the dangers of a larger table opening, prevent heavy cuts.

Make certain openings in between the tables, and also, the reducing head is simple enough to remove the blade.

Do not move around with the wood as it's going through the equipment. Stay on the left side of the equipment beside the front table.

Make sure all knives are sharp and completely balanced

Keep the table free of anything other than the wood

- **Planar**

Make use of drive belts and pulleys with metal guards to prevent accidental contact.

You can avoid kickbacks by not feeding woods of various thicknesses through.

The operant must never stand in the line of board travel.

The exhaust system should always remain in good working order. Safety glasses or face guards shield the operator from bits and chips that may be thrown back by the cutting heads. Hearing protection is also necessary.

If the board gets stuck in the maker, never check the front of the planer. Major eye and face injuries can occur from flying knots and splinters.

Almost remember to use natural leather hand pads, not gloves when taking care of rough lumber. Keep the feed rolls, chip breaker, and pressure bar adequately changed.

- **Sander**

An efficient exhaust system and eye protection is a prerequisite in the sanding process.

Drum sanding preventative measures
 - Set the drum sander for little cuts.
 - If the stock catches on the edges of the bed, stop the machine.
 - Keep your hands off moving machinery.

Disc sanding preventative measures
 - Protect the disc and secure the table properly.
- Sand just on the downstroke of the disc and hold the supply securely versus the bed stop.
 - Keep your hands far from the disc.

Belt sanding safety measures
 - Keep the stock resting securely on the machine bed stop.
 - Hold the sanding obstructs squarely and firmly, as well as away from the belt edges.

- Look out for damaging belts when sanding a tiny, uneven piece.

- **Woodworking lathes**

Safe job habits can prevent most hazards associated with woodturning lathes when the job is finished with hand devices. When using mechanical cutting heads, follow proper operating methods and appropriate guarding.

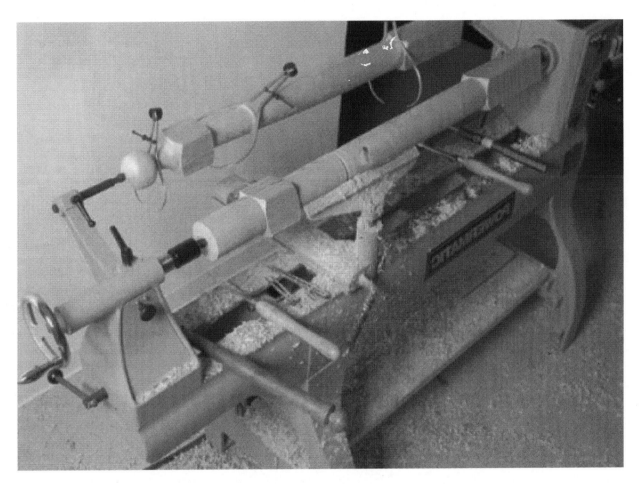

Woodworking Lathe Machine

6. Wood Glue

If there's one material, besides timber, that's key to furnishings; it's timber adhesive.

Since ancient times, the glue has been used to construct furniture, and it's possible to see glued pieces that are centuries old. Take a trip to an art museum and also check out furniture from ancient Egypt or the European Renaissance.

While the purpose of adhesive hasn't changed over the years, the innovation certainly has. Currently, there are several specialized types of glue for all sorts of applications.

The good news is, just a few play a vital role in furniture-making: hide glue, epoxies, and polyurethane.

The earliest glues were hide glues, and these are still in use today. Hide adhesive is made from animal products, and it's valuable for projects like musical tools, where disassembly is frequently needed to make repairs. As warmth and moisture cause hide adhesive to launch its bond, it's relatively easy to separate pieces without harming them.

Hide adhesive likewise works slowly, so it can be an excellent option for challenging joints or building and construction pieces that take a long period to set up.

However, the objective of most furnishing jobs is to create something that can endure exposure to warm and humid conditions. Luckily, today's furniture manufacturers have various alternatives.

Two-part epoxies are possibly the most durable of all adhesives. For scenarios where severe water resistance is called for, epoxy is the most effective choice. Unfortunately, it's pretty challenging and also untidy to use. Epoxies are also poisonous, so you need to don handwear and may even need a respirator to safeguard yourself from direct chemical exposure. These hassles make epoxies a poor option for day-to-day work.

Among the most recent adhesives to show up on the furniture-making scene is polyurethane adhesive, which is intended for just about any gluing job. This adhesive works unlike any other. It actually sets by being exposed to dampness, so it's an excellent choice when wetness resistance is a problem. You also need to wet wood surface areas before applying this adhesive.

This product becomes a foam-like compound as it works and, at the same time, broadens out of the joint. This can make sanding away the glue much harder. Likewise, because it's so brand new, it can't boast the effective long-term record that other glues can.

White Glues and Yellow Glues

One of the most common furniture glues is polyvinyl acetate adhesives, also called white and yellow adhesives. While white glue is a good general adhesive that can be used in a lot of permeable products, yellow glue have been developed explicitly for interior woodworking applications.

Yellow glue is called aliphatic resin glue. Neither of these glues works well if a water-resistant bond is required. They are also not good choices for building things like premium outside doors or outdoor furnishings.

White Glue   Yellow Glue

For these specific jobs, there are waterproof solutions for yellow glue. These are known as cross-linking PVAs(Poly Vinyl Alcohol), as they set via chemical reaction, instead of evaporation.

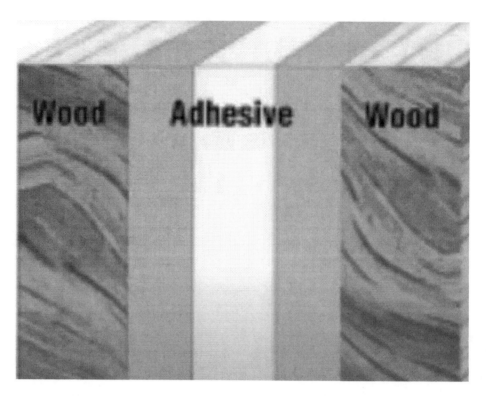

For general woodworking, this adhesive is compatible with standard yellow glue, although it can't be tidied up with water after it has cured.

While each of these products has its place in the furnishing manufacturer's repertoire, an aliphatic resin adhesive is the best choice for a newbie. It's easy to use, does not need mixing, is non-toxic, and cleans up with water.

It likewise sands cleanly, without obstructing the sandpaper, and leaves an undetectable glue line if the joint is limited. Like all adhesives, nevertheless, it does have a limited service life. Once it's open, it's good for about a year.

If you discover that the adhesive has begun to smell sour and seems thick or fibrous, it should not be used.

Gluing Strategies

When preparing a glue joint, keep a couple of guidelines in mind.
- While contemporary glues are strong, if joints do not fit effectively or the glue is not allowed to cure appropriately, the bond will not last long.
- Less glue is better or more appropriate for a strong bond. A slim, even layer of glue will develop a solid bond between two pieces of wood, while thick padding of adhesive does the contrary. A thick coat of glue weakens the joint.

To get an active edge joint, the long mating surfaces have to be held the whole time tightly.

You should not rely on clamps to hold bowed boards together, as this puts excessive stress on the joint.

The fit of a mortise-and-tenon joint should likewise be exact, neither too tight nor too loose.

The parts should fit optimally together. A tighter joint will have no space for glue, whereas if there is excess space, the glue layer will end up too thick. The optimal tightening should ensure a paper-thin layer of glue between the joints. You can use a scrap stick, tiny brush, or a slim roller to do this. Ensure the coverage/spread of glue is full and even.

The mating surfaces also need to be clean, dry, and devoid of contamination before you spread the glue.

Oil, waxes, and certain chemicals like silicone will undoubtedly stand up to the adhesive.
The water can weaken the joint by preventing the bond between wood surface areas.

All glues have a recommended open time, which specifies the amount of time you can leave the adhesive exposed to the air before assembling the joint.

For most yellow glues, this is around 10 minutes. However, the open time will certainly differ with the temperature level and moisture of the environment.

Hot, dry conditions will cause the adhesive to cure quicker. In difficult assemblies, where several joints must be prepared simultaneously, it is essential to factor the open time frame into account.

In some cases, you'll have to complete a job by making smaller subassemblies initially.

Additionally, bear in mind that yellow glue will not perform well in cold conditions.

Many suppliers suggest that both the room and wood surface areas get to at least 55F before applying glue.

Once a joint is assembled, it has to be clamped together. Clamps serve two functions. They draw a joint together securely and also hold it in a fixed place while the glue cures.

You should not apply heavy pressure with your clamps because this will push glue out of the joint.

If the appropriate amount of glue has been spread and a proper quantity of pressure used to tighten up the clamps, you will see small grains of adhesive squeezing out of both sides of the joint.

To eliminate this squeeze-out, let it sit for about 20 mins, and after that, use an old chisel or putty blade to remove the excess.

Some people suggest cleaning the excess adhesive off with a damp cloth. But this should be avoided because it can force adhesive into the surrounding timber pores--particularly with open-grain timbers.

However, this glue will certainly not appear until it's too late to do anything to repair it easily. Finally, yellow glue ought to be permitted to cure for a minimum of an hour before you remove the clamps.

And a full cure takes at least one day, so don't mess with the assembly until this time has passed.

How to Apply Glue							
Glue	Applications	Working Temp	Water Resist	Open Time	Clamp Time	Remarks	Cautions
Regular Yellow	Indoor Projects	50° +	Poor	5 Min	30 Min	Widely available, inexpensive, strong bond.	Freezing can ruin glue
Type II Yellow	Indoor or Outdoor projects	50° - 85°	Excellent	5 Min.	1 Hr	Same as above, plus water-resistant.	Freezing can ruin glue
White	Indoor projects where longer open time is desired	60° +	Poor	8 Min.	1 Hr	Bond is not as strong as yellow glue.	Freezing can ruin glue
Polyurethane	Indoor projects, outdoor projects	50° +	Excellent	20 Min	4 Hr.	Needs moisture to cure. Foams as it cures	It can react with moisture in the skin. Wear gloves

Epoxy	Bonding dissimilar materials (i.e., metal or glass to wood), bonding oily woods, and for waterproof bonds	35° + depending on the formula	Waterproof	5 Min. to 90 Min. depending on the formula	Varies with open time	A two-part system that must be mixed before use	Repeat exposure can cause sensitization. Avoid skin contact, wear a respirator and goggles.
Contact Cement	Plastic laminates and veneers to substrates	65° +	Fair	10 Min. to 60 Min.	Apply pressure with the roller	Solvent-based open time shorter than water-based open time	Vapors can be extremely flammable. Do not use near open flames.
Super Glue	Repairing small cracks, chips, securing inlays	50° +	Very Good	15 Sec. to 5 Min	None	Accelerator available to speed cure times	Bonds on the skin instantly. Fumes may be irritating to the eyes.
Hot Melt Glue	Temporary bonds with easy removal	240° - 400°	Fair	5 Sec.	None	Glue sticks must be heated in the glue gun.	Hot glue dripped on the skin can cause burns
Resorcinol	Waterproof joints	65° +	Waterproof	15 Min.	10 Hr	A two-part system that must be mixed before use.	Powder and fumes are hazardous. Wear goggles, respirators, and gloves when using.

7. Wood Finishing

Wood Finishing Basics

The finishing process involves how to prepare surface areas, how to color them with wood dyes and stains precisely, and how to apply different types of varnish.

There are few essential things to consider.

Before you apply any finish, make sure that your timber is dry, tidy, well sanded, and free from wax and oil. The other thing to keep in mind is that dampness will certainly undo all your good work. To keep water out of your timber, you will undoubtedly require a finish on every surface. If you're working on an outside door or home window, seal any gaps between the timber and masonry after you've used the finish.

There are several essential factors when using a coating-- some visual and some functional. A finish can reduce seasonal activity and also the resulting stress and anxieties on joinery.

It likewise makes a surface area extra impact-resistant and also protects the wood against everyday use, whether the wood item is a cooking area table or an outside chair. Likewise, the right mix of dyes, spots, and clear coatings can turn routine timber into something really unique.

Materials Required
- Varnish, Wood Stain, Dye
- Abrasive paper
- Bucket and sponge
- Cellulose thinner
- Tidy lint-free rag
- Cork sanding block
- Filling knife
- Scrapers
- Varnish and wood stain brushes
- White spirit
- Wire woolen '00' quality
- Wood filler

Using Varnishes, Stain and Dyes

- Tidy the surface area

Dust, oil, and wax will prevent wood stains, varnishes and dyes permeating, or v sticking. Specific stains will need to be wiped over with white spirit or cellulose thinner both before and after sanding.

- Sand the wood

The best way is to sand in phases using a hand or power sander. Remember to sand along the grain. Round off all sharp sides, especially on exterior lumber, as this is where your finish would break up.

- Preservative usage

For exterior timber, apply two layers of preservative, or just one layer for interior work.

Wood Stain

Rather than hiding it, wood stains are used to enhance the all-natural shade of the timber.

There are different types of stains, and selecting the best one can seem like a difficult choice.

Nevertheless, what it truly comes down to is the following:

- it needs to be simple to apply
- it should be compatible with the surface you want
- it has to dry within a reasonable timeframe
- it must keep its color without fading

Many timber stains are made to soak into the timber, although there are exceptions.

Most notably, external wood stains form a thin film externally-- not unlike paint-- to secure the timber.

This is why most stains that you'll find in your neighborhood store are categorized as interior stains, not exterior ones.

However, many indoor stains are appropriate for use outside as long as several layers of varnish are used to subsequently protect the timber.

Water Stains

Water stains come in the form of powder. These are the least expensive of all stains but are not generally offered in huge residential renovation stores. You will likely have to purchase them online

These stains are offered in just a few shades-- Vandyke crystals (brown), mahogany (cozy brown), and also nigrosine

(black)-- are the most common.

To get the exact color you need, you will most likely need to blend the above three

To alter the depth of the color, adjust the powder to water ratio.

Applying a water stain

Apply the stain to the timber with a cloth or paintbrush. A brush is ideal if you are staining carvings, moldings, or any other irregularly-shaped product.

Nevertheless, a cloth holds extra stain and, for flat surfaces, is much easier to use.

Before applying the very first layer of stain, gently wet the timber. This will help to produce an even spread of the stain. Ensure that you have enough for the whole job: it is far better to have to discard the excess than to try and match the previous set's shade precisely.

Do not pour the stain on, but still be generous in its application. Water stains dry extremely gradually, so you should rub-off the excess stain with a paper towel or lint-free cloth.

 Once the stain has dried, use more stain on any areas that are too light.

Keep in mind: water stains may appear to dry within 40 mins, but a second coat should be made only after a minimum of 12 hours.

Oil dyes

Oil dyes usually come blended and are identified by the sort of timber they closely match (such as oak, mahogany, and more). These shade names should be used as a rough overview and shouldn't put you off trying them out.

Using an oil color

Oil dyes can go into the unequal grain, and this can create an uneven coating.

To solve this problem, the timber must be prepared through sanding. A brush or cloth can be used for these dyes.

Alcohol stains

This is a regular stain used by expert woodworkers because of the wide variety of colors available. They are sold as a powder and need to be blended to the ideal shade.

As they are alcohol-based, these stains can likewise be mixed with shellac gloss for color.

Alcohol stains dry extremely quickly (generally in about 5 mins), and so are consequently preferable for spray application.

Nevertheless, the fact that they dry so quickly can also create problems and a patchy finish.

Using an alcohol-based stain

As discussed above, the best method of applying this is with a spray gun. Apply the stain sparingly. You can likewise dip with alcohol stains. The most effective strategy for this is to dip the items in and then leave them immersed for around five minutes.

Pigment stains

This kind of stain is made from finely ground pigments. These do not liquify as dyes do. Pigment stains add a semi-opaque color to the timber and are best used to camouflage the original feel and look of the timber (such as on low-grade lumber).

Using a pigment stain

Use the stain with a brush and be extremely liberal with the quantity of stain used.

Once the whole surface has been coated, wipe off any excess stain with a soft lint-free cloth.

Wax stains

Wax stains are basically a prefabricated mix of wax and also a specific stain. One preferred wax stain is "antique" pine wax. As it is a wax stain, it cannot be used under any other kind of coating, such as shellac. Think of the wax stain as being a short-cut service, integrating the stain and waxing procedure into one.

Applying a wax stain

Use the wax stain as you would a normal finish coat of wax.

8. Ten Woodworking Projects for Beginners

1. Simple Box with Lid

This is a standard method for making a little box using simply a miter box and saw.

Devices and material:
- ruler or measuring tape
- Miter box, and saw or table, saw
- Glue
- Clamps (small).
- Wood: one 4-foot (1x4 piece)
- Sandpaper.

The wood used is standard 1x4 pieces of pine from the neighborhood Home Depot. A sharp observer would keep in mind that the 1x4 is, in fact, closer to 3/4 x 3 1/2. (Remember Nominal vs. Actual size discussed earlier)

Measure and cut:
4 - 7-inch longboards.
2 - 5-inch boards.
1 - 8 1/2 inch board.

Make it as accurate as possible. One-piece of advice would be to measure the next board as per the previous board. Pre-measuring might result in some shorter pieces.

Do not sand any of the edges prior to gluing. It is usual for individuals to want to give it a fast swipe to wipe the edges and such, but what will end up happening is that you will damage the straight side of the board. If you have any chipped edges, smooth it off with your finger; after that, glue it.

Steps

1. Take one 7-inch piece and place a thin layer of wood glue on both of the long edges.

2. Put two more of the 7-inch boards on the glued sides to make a "U" shape. Make sure the ends align and that everything is straight.

3. Clamp ends loosely, to hold together.

4. Put the last 7" board at the top without adhesive and apply a clamp to keep it there. This board is just there to guarantee that the sides are straight and that the top space is not broader than the bottom. Do not trust your eyes on this set.

5. Tighten all the clamps while inspecting the boards to make sure nothing has slid around. If you have a big gluing area, it's not uncommon for the items to move a little. You should see some glue squeezing out. Otherwise, you either have too little a space to use the exact amount of glue needed, or you did not use enough glue.

6. Allow it to cure completely. Do not touch it for an hour, at least.

7. When it looks completely dry, carefully remove the clamps. The joints might still be loose. Set the un-glued 7-inch board aside.

8. Put a slim layer of adhesive on both of the "U" shaped sides.

9. Keep both end caps on, taking care to line up the sides as best you can. The closer you get, the much less you need to sand.

10. Clamp both end caps in position and let the entire point dry overnight.

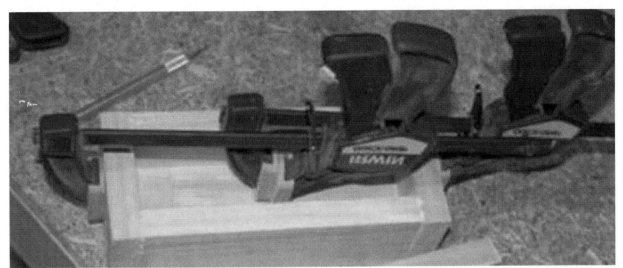

11. Remove the clamps.

12. Take that last 7-inch board and check the fit inside the top. If it's also close, sand the edges until it fits conveniently. If you have difficulty getting it out once again after you have fit it, screw a little screw in the center and use that. As the rest of the top is made, the hole will be covered.

13. Take that 8 1/2 inch board and measure it out and make a line that is 3/4th of an inch from each side. That last 7-inch piece must fit comfortably in between the lines.

14. Glue up one full side of the 7-inch board and put it in lines on the 8 1/2 inch board. Secure tightly. It will certainly be prone to sliding around a little.

When the adhesive dries, un-clamp, and check whether the lid fits.

2. Simple Box with Rabbet Joint

Materials Required:

- Wooden board(regular three-quarter-inch lumber)
- Glue
- Clamps
- Saw
- Router
- Dado Blades
- Miter Gauge

Steps

- Use generic 3/4" lumber for the box. First, cut the items-- 4 sides, the leading and also all-time low. Rip to size by first cleaning up one side, then cutting the other side to the desired size.

- Shave the sides of the lid pieces to align, then glue together. Gently clamp to dry completely. Do not tighten the clamps too much.

- It is time to make a rabbet joint. Drop your table saw blade to ensure that it is just half the width of your board. The area of a "sacrificial board" versus the rip fence so that it can be used against the blade.

- We are also most likely to be utilizing the miter guide for making rabbets; however, please note that you DO NOT want to use the rip fence and even the miter blade with each other if you are doing straight crosscuts.

- To make the rabbets on the sides, start at the edge of the board and make multiple cuts until you get to the rip fence.

- To make the rabbets for an all-time low of the box (along the length of the boards), start with the rip fencing against the saw blade, and gradually move out to the desired dimension.

- Use your board against the bottom piece to get an excellent tidy fit.

- It's now time to fit the boards together. I advise a band clamp for this-- it will be well worth the money. Nevertheless, bar clamps will work if that's what you have.

- Measure the bottom board directly against your box. I make a pencil mark instead of using determining tape.

- Glue the sides as well as the bottom together at the same time to keep everything square.

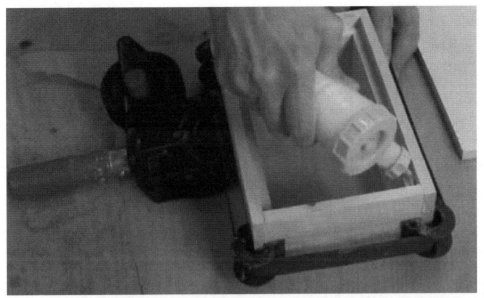

- Secure to completely dry, once again taking care not to tighten the clamps too much.

- When the glue is completely dry, remove the clamps and measure for your lid.

3. IPad Stand

Materials:

- Piece of good timber (130 x 80 x 24 mm or 5.1 x 3.1 x 0.9 inch, if you like).

Devices required:
- Saw.
- Drill.
- Larger diameter drill bit (we use 19mm).
- Sandpaper.

Steps
- Take a wooden block of 130 x 80 x 24 mm

- Pierce a 10mm deep hole in the block. This creates a tiny hole for easy accessibility to the iPad's home button. It is better to do this first.

- Locate the middle of the short side and mark it 17mm to the inside. This will certainly be the facility factor of the little opening. Pierce a hole, around 10mm deep.

- 27-degree angle cut: Make two such cuts, as shown in the figure. This is where your iPad will sit.

- Go 15mm deep and clean it out thoroughly. You can do this by hand or using a handsaw, or go the simple method and use a flexible table saw.

- Smooth it by sanding it down: Make the stand as smooth as you can by fining sand down. Make sure the edges of the little hole are smooth so it won't damage your iPad.

4. Tic- Tac- Toe Game (Noughts and Crosses)

While any woods will work, I advise three types of timber for the job:
- Light Maple
- Oak
- Black Walnut.

Make use of the maple for the trim, the oak for the blocks, and the walnut for the strips. Also, a hand-rubbed linseed oil finish brings out the grains.

Tools:

- Paper, Pen, Set Square
- Wood Piece for Board and scrap wood for O's and X's
- Band Saw, Jigsaw and Lathe for Wood Turning
- Danish Oil, Sanding Tool

Steps

1. Make 2" squares for Crosses.

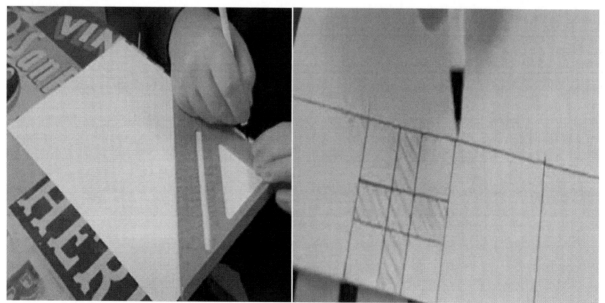

2" square master Cross

2. Cut the crosses. Take out the scrap wood from any firewood pile you have and cut to size, as shown below(for making X's). Cut the wood strip on the band saw.

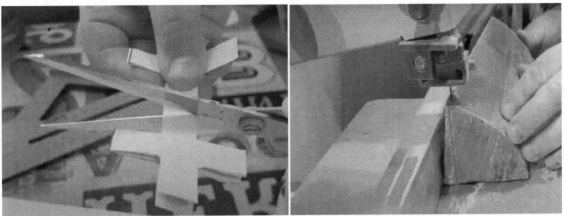

| Paper Crosses | Cut strip of Band Saw |

3. Now, stick the paper template on the wood. Make O's by turning the lathe.

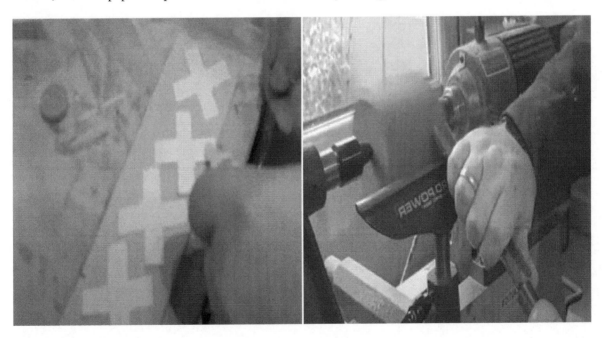

4. Drill the hole and then cut the slices of the cylindrical wood piece.

5. Now cut the crosses which were stuck on the wood piece earlier (using jigsaw). Then sand the X pieces.

6. After sanding, put a coat of Danish oil on the X's and O's and cut out the board. Sand the board and spray white color.

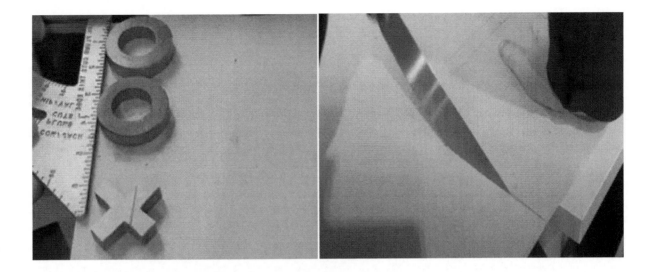

5. Draw boxes on the whiteboard and then put the X's and the O's.

5. Cutting Board

This job can use scrap timber you already have in your workshop.
If you choose brand new wood from the lumber lawn, both hardwoods, as well as softwood, are great selections.

You will need to:
1. Cut the supply
2. Laminate the boards
3. End up the board

Steps

Cut the Stock

1. The block density is determined by the width you cut from the items. For example: For a block to be 111 thick, you will certainly cut the supply 1" wide due to the lamination process, which will group the boards.

2. You can cut the stock a little longer than you desire the size of the cutting board to be. You will cut the board after it has been laminated as well as sanded.

Laminating the supply

1. Use resorcinol adhesive on both sides of the supply to glue them together. Resorcinol adhesive is waterproof and provides stability if the board is soaked in water.
2. After gluing, secure the boards together and let dry overnight.
3. Rub off additional glue before it dries to prevent cracking the cuffing blades when completing as well as forming.

Finishing

- As the board dries, take out of the clamps and use a belt sander to smooth the top and lower surface areas.
- Cut the board to length using a table or circular saw. If you are using a table saw, make sure that the reducing blade does not go beyond 1/4" over the cutting board to prevent drag.
- We are using a shaper or router placed over the edge on the top surface area of the cutting board.
- Use a non-toxic coating such as mineral oil or a salad dish finish for this project.

6. Cactus Planter

Tools:

- Scrap Wood
- Circular Saw
- Miter Saw
- Forstner Bit or Hole Saw

Scrap Wood

Steps

- Take a piece of scrap wood. Plan to cut it into a 90 mm high and 100 mm wide section using a circular saw.

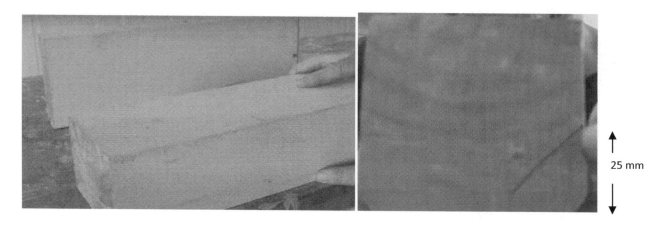

25 mm

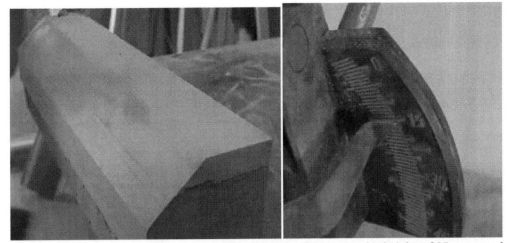

- At the base of the wood, make a line at a 45-degree inclination at the height of 25 mm, as shown in the picture above.
- Next, we have to cut the cactus planter to length (340 mm) using a miter saw, keeping 15 degrees inclination of the saw.

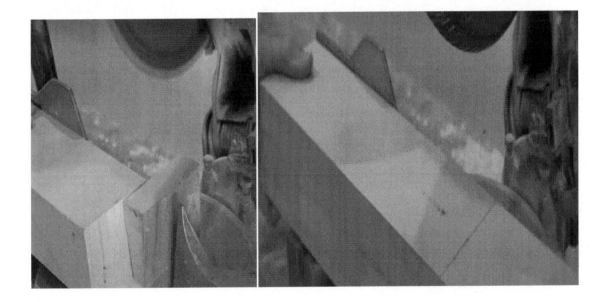

- Use a driller with a Forstner bit to make a hole. Alternatively, you can also use a hole saw. The depth will be 60 mm.
- Now, with a miter saw at 15 degrees as done earlier, cut three pieces of the woodblock with three holes.

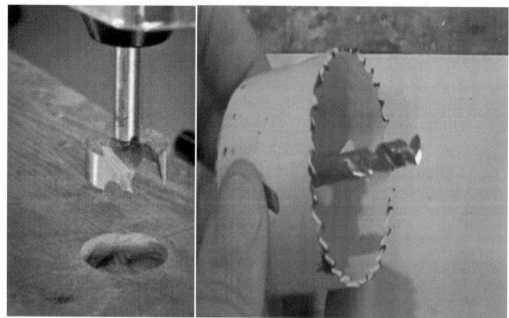

Forstner Bit   Hole Saw

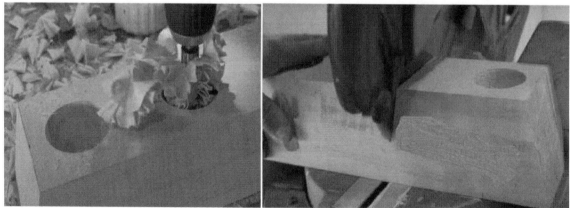

Make holes (60 mm)   Cut into three pieces

- Sand the wood pieces, apply paint, and plant the cactus, as shown below.

7. Candle Holder

Materials & Equipments
- Wood: Find some scrap pieces/sheets of wood, not too thick (< 1/2" is simpler to cut). You need to have at least two colors (better three or more) to blend with plywood.
- Wood adhesive
- Forstner bit: To drill the hole for the required candle size
- Power drill
- A saw: Jig or Table Saw
- Sanding block
- Sandpaper: 60, 100, and 200 (or comparable grits).
- Clear coat and a paint shrub
- Setsquare
- A vice will certainly be valuable but is not necessary
- Some clamps are also helpful but not essential

Dimension Planning
- Ask yourself exactly how big/tall you want the holders, see what dimension the scrapwood permits

- For example, you can make them square, about 3" x 3", if the candles are 1 1/2" in size.

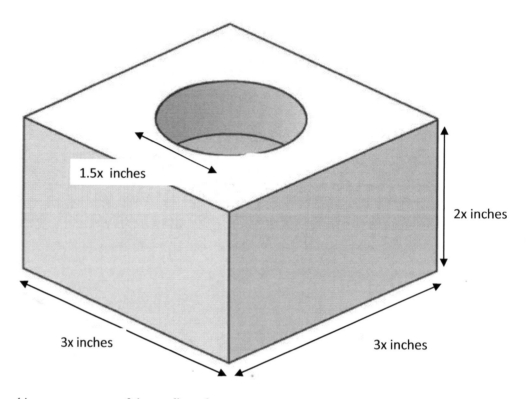

1.5x inches

2x inches

3x inches

3x inches

Cut the wood
- Begin by making a pattern out of the cardboard
- Then use the pattern to trace equal squares on each item of wood.
- Now you cut the wood: use your saw or power tools to cut the squares
- After you've cut the timber, do not sand the edges yet, gluing comes first

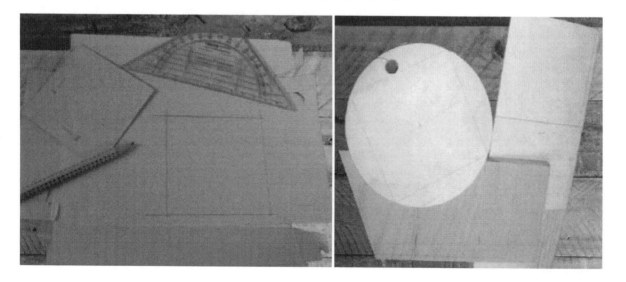

Gluing

- Cut the squares of the desired color; glue them together - on top of each other.
- The glue should be applied in optimum quantity. Both too much and too little glue will impact the strength of the bond negatively.

Sanding

- Relying on how exactly you cut the timber, this process can be really quick or rather slow.
- You start with the roughest paper on the sanding-block to make the four side surface areas flat; after that, you switch to the medium sandpaper and go over the same surfaces.
- While sanding, always check if you have right angles, do that with a set square. Mark the areas were you need to grind even more timber off and do it.
- Use the finest paper to make all the surfaces and sides smooth.

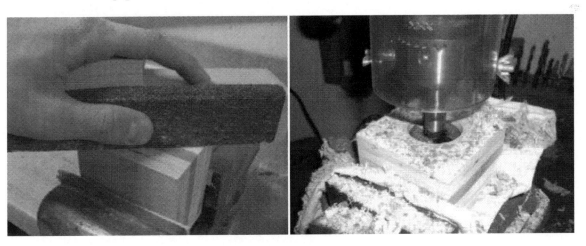

Drilling

- Attach the Forstner bit to your drill.

97

- Make two diagonal lines and locate the center on topmost Square.
- If you only have a hand drill, take care to hold it as upright as feasible, look from different directions to examine if you are.
- After that, use the fine sandpaper again to smooth the edge of the hole.

Paint.
- Use a paintbrush to add the clear layer to the timber - read the instructions on the can/bottle to know when it's completely dry.
- When the initial layer of clear coat is completely dry, utilize 400 sandpaper to smooth the surface areas once more; after that, apply an additional layer of clear coat.
- Let it dry once again.
- You are done!

8. Wooden Cup

Materials & Equipments
- Scrap wood
- Sand belt
- Power drill
- Sandpaper

Steps
Getting the Wood
For your mug, you can use a piece of dead cedar from your backyard.

Shaping

This action is to saw off any projections and make it as semi-round as possible. I used a regular saw and a clamp for this.

Belt Sanding

This following step can be skipped depending on just how symmetrical you cut your burl; however, this makes points less complicated. All I did was run it against the belt
sander to fine-tune the shape a bit more.

Right here's where the mug starts taking shape.

If you do not have a lathe to form the mug, use a drill. Firstly, use a screw and cut off the head with a steel saw.

Then clamp down on this screw with the drill as if it were a drill bit.

Then drive the screw into the middle of the mug. Draw the circle dimension you want the mug to be.

 You then run the drill slowly while holding it in one hand to manage the rate, and, on the other hand, you hold sandpaper up to your cup.

Always keep in mind to put on shatterproof glass and make sure your wood is protected. If you do not, the wood might fly off and hurt someone. Also, use gloves to prevent any injury to your hand.

Removing the center wood

This is one of the most time-consuming components, but this is the only way I could think of with the devices I had readily available. First, I drilled several openings right into the mug to make removing the middle easier.

Make sure you don't pierce too deeply by taping off the drill bit to the size you want to pierce. After that, use a pocket knife. After that, use a Dremel. If you do not have a Dremel, it's likely to take more time.

Next, use fine-grit sandpaper to make the walls of the mug as thin as possible.

Penalty Grit Sanding
You're almost there. Next, simply go over it with grit sandpaper and get it as smooth as you can with the highest possible grit paper.

Completing the Mug
Many surfaces can be made use of, yet I picked walnut oil and beeswax for a couple of factors. Number one being that it develops a waterproof seal for the timber. I got them both online for a couple of dollars.

Generally, I make use of a paper towel to place a layer of walnut oil on the timber, and after that, let it dry overnight. For the mug, I put three layers then smooshed on a layer of beeswax.

9. Wooden Comb

Materials & Equipments
- Scrap wood
- Jigsaw
- Sandpaper
- Beeswax

Prep the Wood

Select the lumber you want to use for this task and prep it by cutting it to size. Run the wood through the planner to get the desired thickness.

Sand

Next, sand your item to the preferred thickness of your comb.

Apply Your Layout/comb design

When your piece has been sanded and cut to its dimension, make use of a stencil of the shape you would like to cut your comb. You can find the stencils on Google by searching "Comb Clip Art" and afterward attached the patterns using spray adhesive.

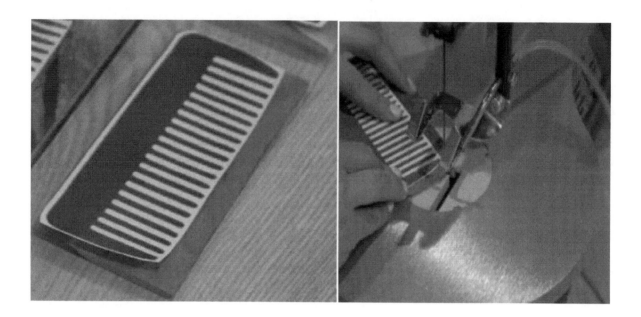

Cut & Forming the Combs.

Cut the combs using a scroll saw or jigsaw and after that sand, form, and fine-tune your combs. You need to work between sanding and engraving bits on a rotary tool to get the final shape.

Complete the Comb.

After your pieces have been formed, sand the item to 400 grit and complete with a **food-safe finish! (Refer below about food-safe finish)**

Food safe finish

1. Mineral Oil.
2. Beeswax.
3. Walnut Oil.
4. Carnauba Wax.
5. Pure Tung Oil.
6. Linseed Oil.
7. Fractionated Coconut Oil.
8. Shellac.

10. Solitaire Game Board

Materials & Equipments

- Free Printable Template
- Router
- 3/4" Forstner Bit
- 1" Core Box Bit
- 1/2" Core Box Bit with Bearing
- Spiral Bit
- Scrap timber with shape -16" x 16" square
- 12" x 12" piece of 1/4" plywood
- Marbles

Print Out the Free Layout

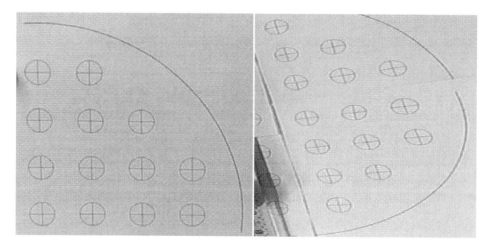

Search for the template online, select whichever you like, and print it out.

Apply glue to the wood blank

You can make use of whatever product you have as long as it is at least 3/4" thick. This would be a terrific opportunity to use up some scraps! Space should be 16" x 16" square.

Use the Printable Layout to Make a Plywood Template

Draw the paper template on a piece of 1/4" plywood. Use a center punch on all the holes to mark for drilling later.

Drill Holes in the Plywood Design template

Using a 3/4" Forstner bit drill with the plywood on all the marks made in the previous step

Make the Outer Well for the Marbles

We are using a 3/4" Forstner bit drill with the plywood on all the marks made in the previous step.

Use a 1" core box bit in a dive router affixed to a circle cutting jig. Establish the bit, so the center of it is 6" from the pivot point of the jig.
Set the depth to cut 1/4" deep, and then take Superficial passes until you reach that deepness.

Cut the Game Board into a Circle

Swap to a spiral bit and readjust the pivot factor of the circle cutting jig to eliminate a 15" circle.

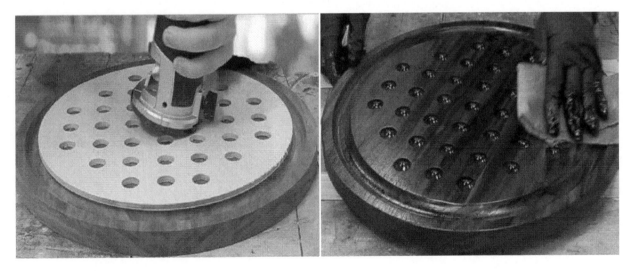

Make the Wells to Hold the Marbles

The following step is to develop all the wells to hold the marbles.

To do this, put the plywood layout on the board, making use of dual-sided tape. After that, use a 1/2" core box bit with a bearing in a router to produce all the little wells in the board. Establish the depth of the bit to cut 1/4" deep, much like the external well.

9. Final Tips and Conclusion

So, how did you find the book till now? I hope that you would have an overall picture of woodworking scope, processes, and tools.

It is a very vast topic with many sub-niches inside it. The practitioners start with a generic approach and specialize in a particular vertical of woodworking.

Before concluding, I would like to discuss a few more critical points, which are about *How to practice woodworking safely while you are starting*. It's like if you have attended Woodworking class, what instructions you would have got in the first few classes!

At the beginning of my woodworking journey, I attended a few preparatory classes. Few learnings remained with me for a long time,

Friend and Enemy Concept

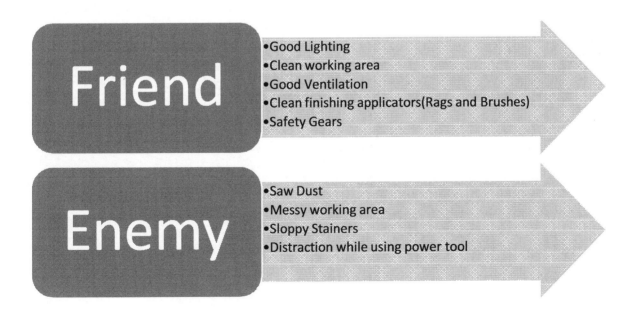

Friend
- Good Lighting
- Clean working area
- Good Ventilation
- Clean finishing applicators(Rags and Brushes)
- Safety Gears

Enemy
- Saw Dust
- Messy working area
- Sloppy Stainers
- Distraction while using power tool

Instructions before starting with any project

- Plan beforehand and then work as per your plan, avoid going with the flow methodology. You should have visualized it before taking the tools. Always rehearse cuts till you are confident and remember the golden rule, "Measure twice or thrice before cutting once."
- Always be focused while using tools, and lack of focus or any kind of distractions can cause injury. Before starting, look for knots or nails in the wood and also avoid using green lumber.
- Do not use your hand to clean up the sawdust, shavings, and scrap material, use a hand brush instead.
- Keep your cell phone off or on mute. The idea is you should not be distracted while using any tool.
- While lifting, do not strain yourself and always keep your back straight.
- Finishing material is highly combustible or prone to catch fire. So use them safely and keep in mind to keep it away from and hot tool or flame. Same tips for rugs and brush applying them.

Using power tools safely

The first safety tip I got was: The safety of the tool is dependent on your focus.

Below are the safety tips for using woodworking tools.

- Always keep machine guards in place
- Remember to have a proper wood size for a cut. A bigger or smaller one can cause an accident.
- Learn proper hand placement: Hold the wood firmly; do not push wood hard towards the blade.
- Watch your fingers and keep them clear.
- Golden Rule: Sharper tools are safe than dull ones: Dull tools require extra pressure, which causes slip and accidents.
- Lastly, learn to engage all your senses with the craft.

This brings the closure of our discussion. I hope you liked the content. I would appreciate it if you could share your feedback and reviews on the platform. You can also reach me at valueadd2life@gmail.com.

Practice safely!

Stephen

10. Appendix

Appendix 1: Woodworking Glossary

- Adhesive: A material that is capable of bonding products together when added to a surface. Glue and contact cement are examples

- Abrasive: Any of the layered papers, textiles, or various other products (including pumice, rottenstone, as well as steel woolen) utilized for smoothing timber or between-coat smoothing of surfaces.

- Acetone - An anemic liquid solvent typically used for cleansing surfaces and the removal of paint and finishes.

- Adze - An axe-like device used to form and appear timber, as well as lumber.

- Aliphatic resin glue - A solid and quick-drying adhesive, more commonly called timber adhesive or woodworker's glue.

- Ampere - A unit of dimension for the electrical present, commonly seen in its abbreviated form (amps).

- Apron - The portion of a table that connects the surface of the tabletop to the legs.

- Arbor - A pin or shaft on which a tool can be connected, such as a router bit or table saw blade.

- Architect's rule (n) - Also referred to as an architect's scale, a triangular ruler with units of measurement marked on each edge.

- Backsaw (n) - A hand saw with an inflexible rib along the rear of the blade, opposite the cutting edge, to avoid bending as well as enable a steady sawing process.

- Band saw (n) - It is a power saw that makes use of a toothed steel blade in a continuous or looped set.

- Bar clamp (n) - A type of clamp with a lengthy bar that extends two clamping jaws, used to hold large products.

- Basswood (n) - A soft, fine wood frequently utilized in sculpting.

- Bevel (v) – Used to cut a piece of timber to a sloped edge; (n)-- an angled piece of timber cut to a dimension besides 90 degrees.

- Biscuit (n) - A small, slice of timber put into holes or ports into items of timber, therefore joining the two.

- Butt joint (n) - A basic, however weak, woodworking joint, generally established as end-grain-to-face-grain, end-grain-to-long-grain or long-grain-to-long grain.

- Cabinet saw (n) - An industrial-grade table saw, usually consisting of a large motor along with trunnion pins attached, and also an enclosed base.

- Cabinetmaker (n) - A professional woodworker that develops beautiful furniture.

- Compound miter saw (n) - This is a power miter saw that rotates on an axis and the arm. Some compound miter saws, called sliding compound miter saws, slide along rails.

- Deal (v) - The process of fixing two pieces of timber together by sawing an adverse profile of one into the other with a favorable account; a term is frequently used in molding.

- Crosscut - This refers to any cut that is made with a vertical positioning to the grain of the wood, the act of making such a cut, and also the wood that has been cut in such a way.

- Cutting checklist (n) - An extensive list of the products required to complete a task, consisting of the names of the needed pieces as well as the measurements of each item, in some cases with a diagram of the boards needed.

- Drawknife (n) - This is a type of blade with a handle on both ends.

- Engineer's Square (n) - Used for showing 90 degrees, an engineer's square is an accuracy steel square with a fixed blade.

- Forstner bit (n) - A tool used to create tidy, flat-bottomed, and also frequently larger holes.

- Grain (n) - Qualities of a timber piece that describes its appearance, figuring, or porosity.

- Groove (n) -A three-sided trench cut into a wood board that is made along the grain.

- Hacksaw (n) - A handsaw, often used for cutting steels, that has a handle at one end and holds at both ends.

- Hand plane (n) - A cutting device used for cutting timber with a blade kept in the area at a steep angle. Hand planes can come in many varieties, including block, bench, bull nose, spokes have, router, scrape, and also rabbet hand planes.

- Jigsaw (n) - A powered, upright, reciprocating blade, used for cutting various products relying on the type of blade utilized. It is called a jigsaw, as it can cut jigsaw puzzles.

- Joinery (n) - The act of connecting pieces of wood with each other. This can be completed in various ways, consisting of using glue and mechanical fasteners or, more typically, by interlacing matching wooden joints.

- Kerf (n) - The excess wood removed by a saw blade in between the timber item and the offcut.

- Kickback (n), unwind (v) - The reverse action seen in woodworking machines when they throw a work surface back in the direction of the operator.

- Lap joint (n) - A joint made use of to enhance a frame edge. Located at either the corner (end lap), in the middle of one piece (T-lap), or in the middle of 2 items (X-lap), this joint deals extra toughness than an enhanced joint, but is weaker than a mortise-and-tenon joint.

- Medium-density fiberboard (n) - Abbreviated MDF, an engineered panel product including wood fibers that are glued under warmth and pressure.

- Miter (n) - The surface area that develops a joint's beveled edge.

- Miter Saw (n) - A power saw that cuts miters, similar to a circular saw.

- Orbital sander (n) - A sander that makes use of the motor's power to develop minute circles, which allows the sandpaper to abrade a surface area.

- Planer (n) - A power device used to plane wood or make the wood piece plane as per the required thickness.

- Points per inch (adj) - A means to identify saw blades (shortened "ppi").

- Rabbet (n, v) - A trench cut into the side of a board that is made up of two-sides.

- Rabbet joint (n) - A basic joint for box structure, allowing for more strength than a butt joint by adding an extra gluing surface area that secures against racking.

- Table saw (n) - A stationary arbor-driven round saw that is housed below the table in which the work piece is cut.

- Tenon (n, v) - A rabbeted side that is utilized by being put into a matching recess, commonly called a mortise.

- Wedge (n) - A small, cut item of wood that is secured in a cut slit in the long run of a predicting item of timber referred to as a through-tenon.

Appendix 2: Adhesives Chart

ADHESIVES CHART

MATERIALS→	Paper	Fabric	Felt	Leather	Rubber	Foam	Styrofoam	Plastic	Metal	Ceramic	Glass	Balsa	Cork	Wood
Wood	W	C/W	Sp/C	W/C/Ca	C/Ca	C	2K/H	L/C	2K/C/L	C/Ca	C/Ca	W	W	L/W
Cork	H/W	H/L	W	Ca/C	Ca/C	2K	W	L/Ca	C/Ca	L/Ca	Si	W	W	
Balsa	W	H/W	W	Ca/C	C/Ca	C	2K/H	L/Ca	2K/Ca	L/Ca	C/Ca	W		
Glass	A/W	A	A	A/Ca	Ca	Sp	2K/Sp	C/L	2K/C	2K/C/L	2K/L			
Ceramic	A/H	Ca/A	Ca/A	Ca/A/C	C/Ca	A	Ce/C	L/Ca/C	2K/C/L	Ce/Ca				
Metal	A/H	A	C	C/Ca	C/Ca	C	2K/H	2K/C	2K/C					
Plastic	H/Sp	Sp/C	Sp/C	Sp/Ca	C/Ca	Ca	Ca/C	L/Ca/2K						
Styrofoam	Sp/C	A/H	Sp	A	L	L/A	A/Sp							
Foam	Sp	Sp	Sp	C	C	Sp								
Rubber	Ca/C	A/C	C	Ca	Ca									
Leather	F/Sp	F	2K	C/F										
Felt	A/H	F/H	H/F											
Fabric	A/H	F/H												
Paper	A/W													

A All-purpose-glue
F Fabric glue
Sp Spray adhesive
H Hot glue
C Contact adhesives
L Construction adhesive (Liquid Nails, Loctite)
Ce Ceramic glue
Si Silicone
W Wood glue
Ca Cyanoacrylate (super glue)
2K Two-component adhesive

Appendix 3: Sources of Free Design/Layout/Project Ideas

1. https://www.rockler.com/free-woodworking-plans

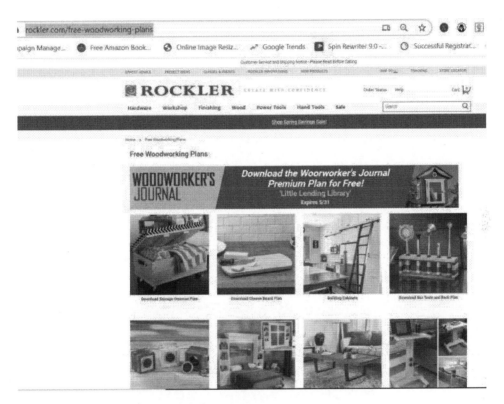

2. https://www.woodsmithplans.com/free-plans/

3. https://www.thesprucecrafts.com/free-woodworking-plans-for-your-home-and-yard-1357146

4. https://www.canadianwoodworking.com/free-plans

5. https://www.finewoodworking.com/blog/free-woodworking-plans

Wood Joinery for Beginners Handbook

The Essential Joinery Guide with Tools, Techniques, Tips and Starter Projects

Stephen Fleming

Bonus Booklet

Thanks for purchasing the book. In addition to the content, we are also providing an additional booklet consisting of Monthly planner and Project Schedule template for your first project.

It contains valuable information about woodworking and leathercraft.

Download the booklet by typing the below link.

http://bit.ly/leatherbonus

Cheers!

Table of Contents

1. Preface

This is the fifth book in my DIY series after the ***Woodworking for Beginners Handbook.*** This book takes the discussion about woodworking a step further with a focus on various types of joinery and their applications.

When I first started woodcraft, I was desperately looking for a go-to guide about the processes and tools I would need.

The content I found online was total information overload and wasn't even presented sequentially. The books I looked at were either focused on just a few processes or assumed that I already had the necessary information. A lot of the books were also very dated.

There are two ways of learning; one is learning from SMEs (Subject Matter Experts) with years of experience, and the other is people who are just a few steps ahead of you in their journey.

I fall into the latter group. I'm five years into this hobby and still learning from the experts.

I still remember the initial doubts I had and the tips that helped me.

This book is for those who are still running their first lap (0-3 years) in wood crafting and want to have a holistic idea of the processes and tools they will need for joinery. The book also discusses Japanese and CNC joinery.

I have included photographs of realistic beginner projects, and I will explain the process and standard operating procedures associated with them.

In the last chapter, Appendix, I have provided a glossary of joinery terms.

Cheers, and let's start the journey

Stephen Fleming

2. Basics of Joinery

What is Joinery? A Definition

Joinery is a fundamental part of woodworking that can be found practically everywhere in the making of furniture, windows, doors, and floor coverings.

Although the vital function of joinery is to **hold wood together** firmly, it can additionally be used to make the wood piece more attractive.

Joinery can either involve a simple process of wood being toenailed or glued together or, it can entail a far more complex joining of two pieces of wood.

The team evaluating joinery technique

118

Here are a few definitions to make things more clear:

- *Joinery is a part of woodworking that involves **joining together pieces of wood or lumber,** to produce more complex woods.*
- *Some wood joints **employ fasteners, bindings, or adhesives,** while others use only wood elements.*
- *The characteristics of wooden joints - **strength, flexibility, toughness, appearance,** etc. - derive from the properties of the materials involved and the purpose of the joint.*
- *Therefore, different joinery techniques are used to meet differing requirements.*

Refer: (https://en.wikipedia.org/wiki/Woodworking_joints)

Carpentry vs. Joinery

Many people are uncertain about the difference between a joiner and a carpenter. If you need a task to be completed, that involves wood, who do you call?

Both carpenters and joiners share numerous qualities; nevertheless, they are described differently, depending on your area - the south of England tends to use the term 'carpenter,' while the north of England tends to say 'joiner.' Both a carpenter and a joiner are tradesmen within the building and construction sector, and both primarily work with wood.

Joiners

A joiner is an artisan who makes or **joins the wood**, generally **in a workshop**, whereas a carpenter constructs wooden pieces **on-site**. In straightforward terms, a joiner makes the timber that a carpenter then fixes on-site. A joiner, therefore, is generally connected to making doors, windows, staircases, and equipped furnishings that are usually made in a workshop off-site because heavy machinery is needed.

Carpenters

A carpenter is typically an expert in more prominent aspects, such as building sand fitting roofing trusses, stud work, and floors on-site by cutting as well as fitting pieces together, making use of a range of materials and devices. Carpenters are accountable for **setting up and building a structure**.

Bespoke Joinery

Bespoke relates to creating something based on someone's unique specifications. Store-bought furniture such as closets, shelving systems, TV systems, and even closets can't be personalized and so won't be tailored to the nuances of a room. Custom joinery also adds value to your home.

Brief Introduction to the Joinery Process

Joinery entails attaching wood pieces of timber. Types of joints involve:

Fasteners
- Screws (open, plugged, capped).
- Pocket screws.
- Nails (hammer and also pneumatic).

Bindings
- Metal straps, metal corners, corners.
- Material straps: fabric, natural leather.

Adhesive
- Wood adhesive: Glue creates a more robust attachment.
- Water swelling.

Wood aspects
- Dowel: A wooden rod set right into both blocks of adjoining wood.
- Biscuit: A small wooden biscuit formed piece is set into both pieces of adjoining wood.
- Spline: Comparable to the biscuit, however, the "spline" runs the joint's whole size.
- Corner blocks: Square or triangular blocks positioned at a joint to attach both blocks of wood.

Commonly used joints in woodworking:

Butt joint: A piece of timber is joined to another part of the wood. This is the simplest, as well as the weakest joint.

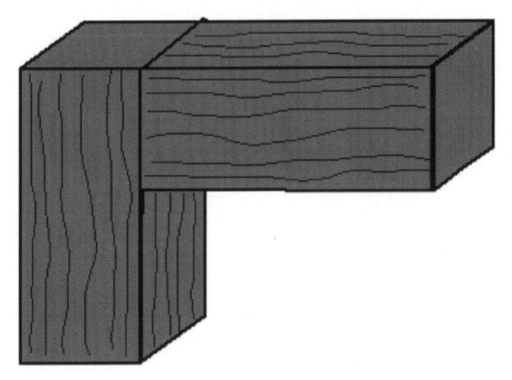

Butt Joint
(Photo Reference: Jomegat at the English Wikipedia / CC BY-SAhttp://creativecommons.org/licenses/by-sa/3.0/)

Miter joint: Comparable to a butt joint, the only difference being both pieces have been placed at a 45-degree angle.

Miter Joint

Lap joints: One wood of wood will overlap the other, as shown below.

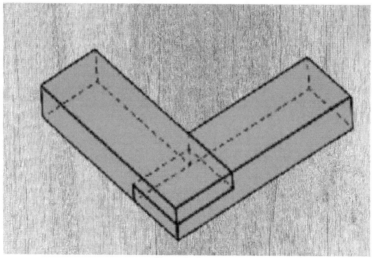
Lap Joint

Box joint: Also called a finger joint, this is used for the edges of boxes. It includes several lap joints at the ends of two boards.

Box or Finger Joint

Dovetail joint: A kind of box joint where the fingers are secured via diagonal cuts.

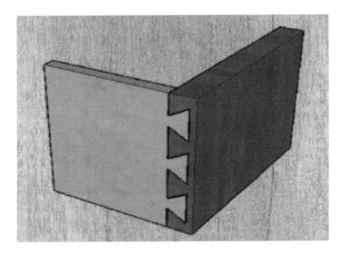

Dovetail Joint

Dado joint: A port is cut across the grain in one piece for another piece to slip into it. Shelves in a bookcase have ports cut into the sides, for instance.

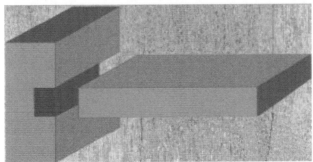

Dado Joint

Groove joint: The port is cut with the grain. After that, one piece is fixed with the other along the grooves.

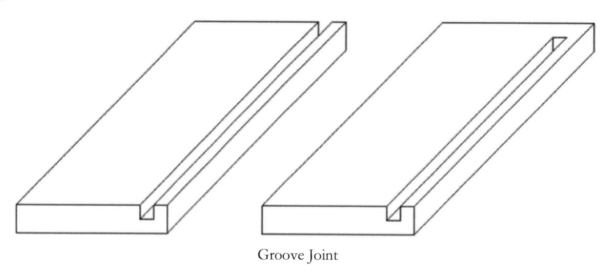

Groove Joint

Tongue and also groove. Each wood has a groove cut entirely along one side, and a narrow, deep ridge (the tongue) is on the opposite side. If the tongue is unattached, it is a spline joint.

Mortise and Tenon

Mortise, as well as tenon: A stub (the tenon) will fit snugly into a hole cut out for it (the mortise). This is a feature of Mission Style furniture and is also the traditional approach to the jointing framework and panel participants in doors, windows, and closets.

Wood Squaring

For wood to be correctly joined, crucial actions have to be taken to guarantee optimal strength as well as integrity, appropriate symmetry, and visual aesthetics. One of these is done by **squaring the wood**.

Natural wood defects

Wane: This is the visibility of bark or the absence of wood fiber along the edges of a wood piece. It doesn't impact the strength of the wood. Nonetheless, it is restricted in framing lumber because of the loss of a nailing side.

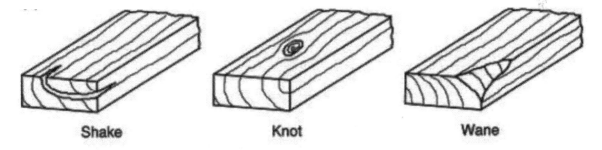

Shake   Knot   Wane

Shake: It is a longitudinally split in the wood, which occurs between or through the yearly growth rings. Shake often happens because of the tree shaking in the wind.

Knot: One of the most noticeable grading attributes is a knot, which is an imperfection in the wood. Knots affect the strength of wood.

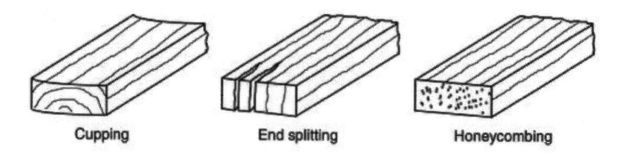

Seasonal Defects

Hole: If a knot develops through the piece of lumber, it creates an opening. Openings can likewise be created by natural creatures or during the manufacturing process. The opening can either extend totally through the timber or just partly, which is then usually described as a surface pit. A hole and a knot of the same size will affect the wood in the same way.

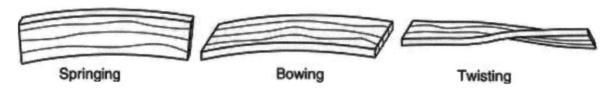

Seasonal Defects

Squaring the timber:

The term "square" describes a perfect 90 ° angle. To put it simply, every face of the lumber is 90 ° to the surrounding side. When wood is aligned, if it is square, the two kinds of wood will create ideal angles to one another.

No light should be visible between boards. This assures that the adhesive is appropriately sealed without any gaps.

Squaring timber starts with the jointer. Plane the faces initially, then the side. As soon as one side is planed, use the table saw to square the last edge. As soon as the sides of the two woods of lumber are squared, you can begin gluing.

Lining up the grain:

When gluing two blocks of wood together along the side, use alternate end grain patterns. This protects against the constructed wood cupping.

126

3. Tools of Joinery

Fasteners

A metal fastener is a type of tool, such as a nail or screw, which joins or affixes two or more woods together. The most common steel fasteners used in woodworking joinery are:

1. Nails (hammer and also pneumatic).

2. Timber Screws (open, connected, topped, putty).

3. Bolts.

4. Pocket screws.

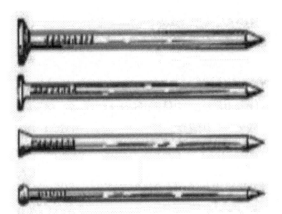

Type of Nails: Top to Bottom: Usual/General, Box, Casing, Finishing

Nails:
There are many types of nails you will use in woodworking: Two of them are:

- Usual/General Nails
- Finishing Nails

General nails have a flat head and used in construction projects.

Finishing nails have a little head and are designed for "punching" or penetrating the wood with a device called a hole strike. By doing so, the nail is pressed right into the timber, and putty is applied over it. This "filler" hides the nail from view and also helps to preserve the all-natural color of the timber.

Wood Screws:

Unlike the smooth shanks of many nails, screw fastenings have a threaded shank with machined spirals shaped in away that the screw might be inserted or removed by turning the head.

There are two typical thread types, coarse threaded as well as fine threaded. Coarse threaded spirals are further apart as well as much deeper than fine threaded spirals and ought to be used in softwoods.

As hardwood grain is a lot more compressed, fine threaded screws should be used.

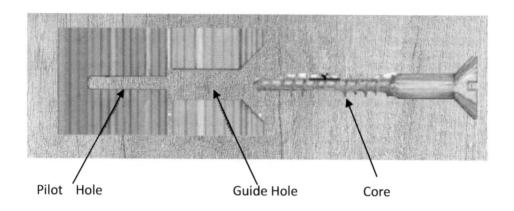

Pilot Hole   Guide Hole   Core

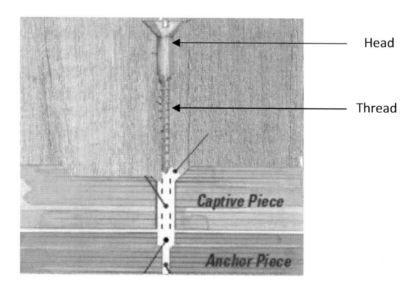

Bolts:

Bolts aren't like screws or nails as they are not driven into the timber. Instead, the hole as per the dimension of the bolt must be pierced in both wood pieces to be joined

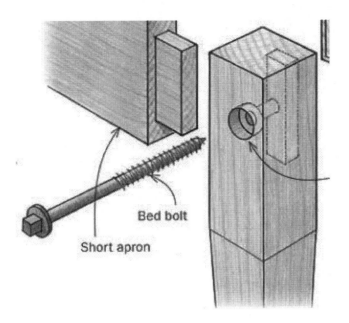

Bed bolt

Short apron

Pocket Screws:

Pocket screws get their name from the fact that they are recessed into the timber in an angled countersink called a pocket. They offer fast, solid, and uniformly matched joinery.

There is little difference between a pocket screw and a basic timber screw, though the head is larger and not tapered, and the screw tip is made to self-tap.

Pocket openings are built using a jig - a device used to hold wood.

Pocket Screws

Splines and Rods

Wooden rods or splines might also be placed, glued, and afterward secured together to provide toughness to wood joints.

Standard rods, as well as spline joints, are:

- **Doweled joints:** A wood rod, called a dowel, is placed and glued in both blocks of wood and then clamp. In the old days, water was used rather than glue. This is because water causes timber to swell, so the dowel would certainly swell in the timber as well as safeguard it.

- **Biscuit joints:** After cutting a slot right into the two blocks of wood to be joined, an oval-shaped, highly-dried, and pressed wood biscuit (generally constructed from beech wood) is

130

covered with adhesive and also put in place. The boards are then clamped together until the attachment is full.

- **Spline joints:** A spline is a thin piece of timber inserted right into two matching ports cut into timber joints, much like a biscuit. A spline is typically added to beautify the job.

Glue and Clamps

131

Clamping and gluing is the process for attaching wood with the force and adhesion necessary to ensure strong timber joints.

This is completed by utilizing clamps and wood glue. Remarkably, when the wood is glued together, it develops a stronger-than-wood bond.

This fact alone makes gluing a valid alternative to consider when sticking timber together.

Various other techniques might be used to help in the process, such as biscuits, dowels, nails, and screws, but an adequately glued butt joint is not to be underestimated.

The Gluing Method:

Before gluing, make sure you have all the necessary devices and tools on the table with you.

First, decide what type of clamp you will use. A clamp is a tool used for holding two pieces of wood together.

There are many different types of clamps, and all of these vary in the level of pressure they can apply.

Different Clamps

Below are the most popular wood clamps:

- Bar clamp
- Timber clamp or hand screw clamp
- C-clamp
- Spring clamp
- Screw clamp
- Strap or band
- Screw clamp
- Toggle clamp
- Pipeline clamp
- One-handed bar clamp
- Miter clamp

The type of clamp you select will be based on the dimension and the amount of pressure you require. Pipeline clamps, for example, are long and have the greatest cranking power. On the other hand, spring clamps are small and have less compression strength.

As soon as you have identified the clamp for your task, you just need to go out and get it. A clamping device is any type of gadget helpful for the gluing procedure.

Below are some clamping tools:

- **Cauls:** Stiff wood planks that are clamped to panel glue-ups, on top of each other, to maintain the specific boards' alignment.

- **Wax paper**: Prevents wooden woods from sticking to the table.

- **Squares**: Allow you to see if the wood is square (90 °).

- **Wet paper towel**: Excess glue is the enemy!

4. Types of Joinery- Detailed Discussion

1. Butt Joint-Basic

Butt joints are one of the most basic approaches for connecting two pieces of timber. Also, while it isn't the toughest of joints, it is useful in some situations.

You can find out exactly how to make a butt joint by utilizing the correct strategy to guarantee that your butt joints are as strong as possible.

As shown in the picture, a butt joint is where one piece of wood is butted against another and joined with adhesive.

Screws or nails typically enhance the joint.

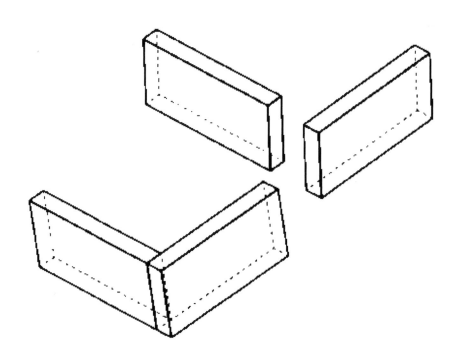

Basic Butt Joint

Square Cuts Are Key:

The trick to a top-quality butt joint is to ensure that the two boards are cut as square as possible. This is best done with a miter saw, although top-quality results can be obtained utilizing a circular saw and a design square, provided that the angle of the blade of the round saw is set to zero degrees.

Types of Butt Joint

Glue Offers Strength:

The strength of a butt joint comes from the glue in the joint.

However, there are two issues with using glue as the only method of holding the connection together.

Initially, when the glue is applied to the end grain of a board, it tends to saturate right into the wood far more than glue on the side of the grain. The end grain is the most porous part of the wood, so you might need to apply a little bit more adhesive.

If utilizing hardwood for your task, make sure to pre-drill the pilot holes before placing screws into the joint.

General Strength of the Butt Joint

The strength of the joint depends on the straightness of the side (not necessarily the squareness) and the positioning of the timber fibers.

This joint doesn't require any type of machine used on its parts. The only preparation required is the planing or jointing of the sides for straightness.

135

With modern adhesives, this joint can be as strong as the timber itself.

One benefit of the butt joint is speed. Nevertheless, without a way to join the two edges for a level joint, you're limited to putting together pieces no longer than 48 inches.

Ways to make butt joint stronger

- Use support from iron; edge pieces are readily available in any equipment shop.

- T plates are excellent if your pieces are out of sight.

T-Plate   Plywood Gusset

- The plywood gusset is likewise an excellent strengthener for butt joints.

- This joinery strengthener is especially useful if you make boxes and cabinets.

| Wooden Block | Corner Brace |

- A woodblock is commonly used to make table structures stronger.

- It is a straightforward method to make your edges with butted joints sufficiently solid to sustain table legs.

2. Mitered Butt Joint

A butt joint is basic and involves wood pieces that are joined at 90 degrees. It isn't one of the prettiest of joints, though, as completion grain of one of the two boards will be visible.

Mitered Joint

When you want something that looks nicer, try a mitered butt joint.

137

It will not be any more durable than a conventional butt joint, but you will also not see the end grain.

Angles need to be specific:

Like with a fundamental butt joint, the most crucial element of producing a mitered butt joint is to cut the angles correctly. For this, you'll need a compound miter saw.

The first step is to figure out the joint's final angle and divide it by two. For a square link (90-degrees), you'll need to make a 45-degree angle cut on both boards to allow joining.

If the two pieces are the same width, the two edges should join flawlessly.

This joint could be used while building various other joints of other angles. As an example, if you were making an octagonal-shaped image framework, each of the eight edges would be 45-degrees (instead of the 90degrees in the previous instance). Thus, you would cut 22 1/2- degree angles on each end to create the butt joints.

Glue holds the joint:

Just like with an essential butt joint, adhesive holds the joint together.

Nonetheless, both sides of the adhesive joint will be on permeable end grain. You will likely need to use even more woodworking glue than when gluing on side grain.

TIP: Dry-fit your pieces before using adhesive to be sure of the final fit. For example, if you're making a picture frame, cut all lengths and angles, then cross-check the structure so that there is no gap between the wood pieces.

Example of furniture using Mitered Joint

Use mechanical bolts for strength:

Similar to a standard butt joint, there isn't a great deal of strength in a mitered butt joint.

So, you might want to reinforce the joint using nails, brads, or screws to provide lateral strength to the joint.

If using hardwood, pre-drill before mounting screws to avoid splitting.

3. Spline Joint

A spline joint is created when a wood spline is placed and glued into the slot or groove of another woodworking joint, usually a butt, side, or mitered joint.

The spline serves to reinforce the joint and keep both areas aligned. This small enhancement adds substantial strength to whatever joint it's used on.

The spline is made from plywood, hardwood, or the exact same material as the joint being strengthened. For the ultimate in toughness, the natural wood grain needs to be oriented to make sure that it's aligned up with the joint on the work surface.

Splines should never ever be pushed into the grooves, which can cause them to misshape or divide. Rather, they must slide in quickly, however, with no side play, to enable adequate space for the glue to create a solid joint.

Miter spline

The miter spline is excellent for strengthening picture frameworks, mirror frames, and cabinet face frames that utilize mitered corners. Tiny appealing boxes can use contrasting tinted splines with mitered edges for visual effect, in addition to strengthening the joints.

The splines are typically no greater than a third of the total thickness of the workpieces. It's ideal for cutting the spline oversize and then trimming and sanding smooth once the adhesive has dried. A dry-fit before glue-up is recommended.

Spline between Miter and at corner slot

Miter spline joints look fantastic when utilizing contrasting colors. A light tinted spline set in a darker wood will certainly attract the eye and also highlight the joint.

Side spline

Edge splines are typically used to make larger panels out of several narrower boards.

The most common side spline joint has the groove and spline running along the wood piece.

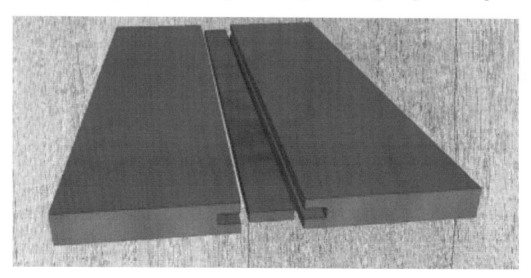

If the look isn't that important, plywood makes an outstanding spline. If appearance is your main concern, the spline can be made from solid timber of your choice.

The stopped edge spline is similar to a quit dado joint because the groove is cut short of the completion of the board, although on both ends in this situation.

140

It is generally used for the tops of hardwood tables as well as various other types of furniture for which the craftsman would like the additional strength.

A simple plywood spline can be used without impacting the appearance of the joint.

As we know, the groove can be cut with a table saw, this is possibly much easier than using a router table with a slotting bit.

The utility of Spline Joint

The purpose is to reinforce as well as straighten the edges. A spline can be used as a substitute for the tongue and groove.

- Splines for toughness: Splines are commonly used to strengthen miter and butt joints

- Splines as accents: Dress up a joint using contrasting timbers

- The framework of the joint: Use the right proportions to ensure toughness and security

4. Half-Lap Joint

These are among the most basic of woodworking joints. There are times where they are the best option for joining two wood pieces together.

A half-lap joint is where two blocks of wood, of the same density, have half of the wood removed to ensure that no thickness is added at the joint.

These joints function well for right-angle links. Both boards have material removed so that they join seamlessly.

When to utilize half-lap joints:

Half-lap joints function well when using one to a two-inch thick wood, such as in dressers & work desks, especially where drawers will be set up.

The half-lap includes strength to the interior and a framework without adding additional height. The half-lap joint can be reasonably strong when used properly.

Nonetheless, be advised that thin pieces of wood might deteriorate in strength after cutting half of the lap to make this joint. So, use this joint when the wood is thick to preserve the stability of the board after half of the wood is removed.

141

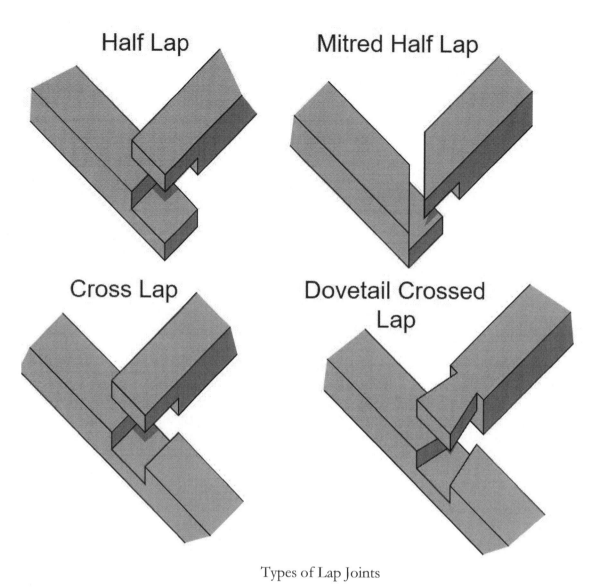

Types of Lap Joints

How to cut half-lap joints:

Many devices can be used to cut half-laps. However, my favorite is a piled dado set on a radial arm saw.

142

You'll need a couple of pieces of scrap wood to get the set perfect, but once you have the appropriate elevation setting on the radial arm, you'll be making plenty of half-lap joints in a short time.

In the absence of a radial arm saw, you can achieve the same with a dado set on a table saw.

Make sure to utilize your miter scale to guide the wood through the blade.

Never use the fence on the table saw for crosscuts, as the fence can make the wood bind.

When you have a cut every quarter inch between the edges of the joint, use a hammer to clean up the thin pieces.

After finishing up the joint with a chisel, you must have a wholly developed half-lap joint.

Putting together the joint:

When you're ready to set up the joint, put some woodworker's glue on both mating surfaces.

Put the other wood of wood in place and adjust both to their final placements. Then, join the wood pieces with a few wood screws.

The adhesive will be the strength of the joint, but the screws are needed to hold it together until the glue dries.

5. Tongue and Groove Joint

The tongue and groove joint is a joint attached edge to edge with two or more pieces of wood.

It is made with one side being composed of a slot that runs down the length of the wood and a tongue that fits into the slot.

Groove   Tongue

This groove and tongue feature allows a stable and aesthetically pleasing joint that can be used in floorboards, lining boards, wood paneling, and tabletops.

This joint type is simple and enables a limited fit that has a lot of area for adhesives.

These joints can be tough to make without the right machinery. You are more likely to purchase wood with this joint already in it, such as lining boards.

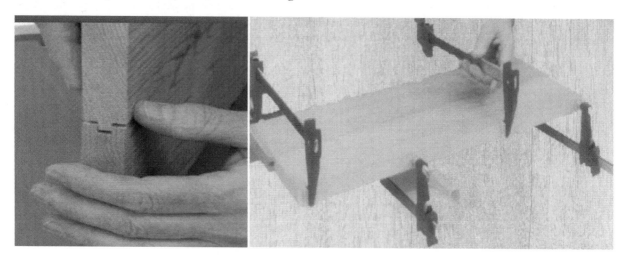

Check Fitment Glue and Clamp

Additionally, this is used more as a function in furniture, so it doesn't typically require a lot of timber.

Step 1: This joint is only used in timber boards. Therefore, the first thing to do is to gauge and cut up some boards of the appropriate length.

Step 2: This step is not entirely essential if you have some experience using a router, but otherwise, you need to note the wood and to get ends on your boards.

Step 3: This action requires a router bench to produce an effective joint, and the first thing you should do is begin with a router bit to reduce the groove. After the groove has actually been made, use an extra router bit to cut the tongue.

Step 4: See if the joint fits tightly, and if it does, you can add adhesive and clamp the boards together, which will interlace your tongue and groove joints.

Tip: The lining boards already have a tongue and groove joints, which makes this option much easier for individuals with time restraints or unskilled woodworkers.

Gluing: The suggested adhesive for drifting installment is tongue and groove engineered floor covering adhesive. Glue placement is critical. The adhesive needs to be positioned along the groove's topside, the complete size of the grooved side, and the end.

An additional **advantage** of this joint is the adhesive surface availability. The single **disadvantage** might be that the joint is visible from the end of the panel. The tongue-and-groove joint is usually used to make wider panels from narrower boards, such as when constructing **tabletops, doors,** or **architectural paneling.**

6. Mortise and Tenon Joint

The mortise and tenon joints have been used for centuries by woodworkers due to their combination of superior toughness and simplicity.

They are usually used when one wood of wood is joined with various others at 90-degree angles but may be used at a somewhat lower angle in certain conditions. Remember that the joint is toughest when the two blocks of wood are at right angles to each other.

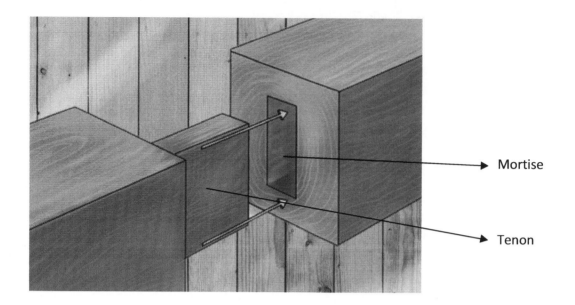

The key behind a mortise and tenon joint is that a piece of wood is inserted right into the other and held in place with a fastener.

Today, a lot of woodworkers use adhesive to safeguard the tenon inside the mortise, but in years passed, woodworkers would style the tenons to make sure that a wedge or dowel protects them.

Making Tenon:

A rectangle pin cut from the end of the wood is tenon.

While tenons can be cut by hand, contemporary woodworkers will typically use a band saw, or a tenoning jig on a table.

When cutting a tenon, beware not to remove excess material, as thinner tenons lead to weak joints.

Cutting the Mortise:

Generally, mortises were cut into the receiving piece of wood using a chisel. Today, several woodworkers use a mortise, which uses a little drill bit encased in a four-sided sculpt.

Several drill press suppliers offer optional mortising attachments, making the drill press a far more functional machine.

To cut a mortise, note where to cut, and after that sink the bit right into the material, taking little bites at a time.

Establish the depth enough to include the entire length of thereon, make it no deeper than absolutely needed (unless you are developing a through-tenon). When completed, use a sharp chisel to clean up any remaining rough spots.

Joint Fitting:

When the mortise and tenon have both been completed, dry-fit the tenon into the mortise.

The fit has to be snug, but not too limiting. As soon as all joints have been formed and its time for setting up, use glue on both the tenon and inside the mortise. Cover all surface areas equally using a tiny brush.

A good rule of thumb when developing mortise, as well as tenon joints, is to cut the mortise first. Keep the tenon bit wider for the dry test of the joint.

Double Mortise Tenon Joint

When this joint is used:

Mortise &tenon is typically used when corner joints require tough frameworks for making things such as doors, tables, home windows, and beds.

A rectangular slot is described as a mortise cut, and it is cut into the (specific) center of the end piece of timber to ensure that it will take in the protrusion fitting (the tenon), thus making a clean, solid joint.

After it has been glued and well equipped, the wood joints will not ove and will be really tough to pull apart.

To ensure that the mortise is one-third as thick as the timber, it has to have precise measurements.This is to avoid any kind of splitting of the mortise and tenon breakage.

7. BiscuitJoint

In comparison to joints such as edge-to-edge joints, miter joints, T-joints, and edge joints, the most effective is biscuit joints.

Properly-cut biscuit joints are reliable as well as precise, particularly when cutting slots with a woodworking device called a biscuit joiner (or plate joiner).

What is a biscuit?
A thin, oval-shaped wood piece, typically made from beech wood, is called a biscuit.

When glued into slots precisely cut by the biscuit cutter, the dampness from the adhesive causes the biscuit to swell and tighten up the joint.

Tools Required for making Biscuit Joint

- A plate jointer, also known as a biscuit jointer.
- A saw.
- Measuring tape.
- Square.
- Wood glue/ Woodworker's adhesive.
- Clamps.
- Lumber.

Different sizes of Biscuits

Biscuits are commonly found in three sizes:
- **0 - 5/8" x 1-3/4"**
- **10 - 3/4" x 2-1/8"**
- **20 - 1" x 2-3/8"**

Biscuit cutters must have the capability to cut all three sizes precisely.

What Size Biscuit to Utilize?

As a basic guideline, using the biggest biscuit will offer the highest amount of toughness to the joint.

Most of the time, use # 20 biscuits. However, when working on narrower material, use a button to smaller biscuits.

Edge-to-Edge Joints:

One of the most typical biscuit joints is edge-to-edge joints. This is typically used for gluing tabletops of varying sizes of the same thickness, where biscuits are used along the long sides of the boards.

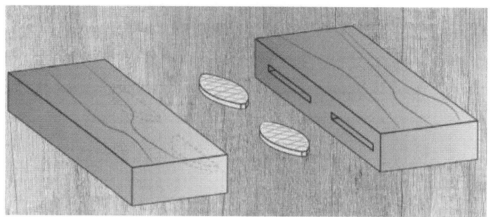
Edge-to-Edge Joints

To glue a tabletop of different boards, lay the boards side-by-side with each board's end grain turned opposite to the previous board. This will keep the tabletop stable if the boards expand or contract.

Once the boards are in the correct positions, use a pencil to make marks across the joints every 4-6". These will be the centerlines for the biscuit ports.

Next, adjust your biscuit joiner depending on the size of a biscuit. In the case of edge-to-edge joints, you'll most likely use the large # 20 dimension.

Place the overview fence on top of the wood (perpendicular to the edge) and straighten the cutting guide with the pencil mark.

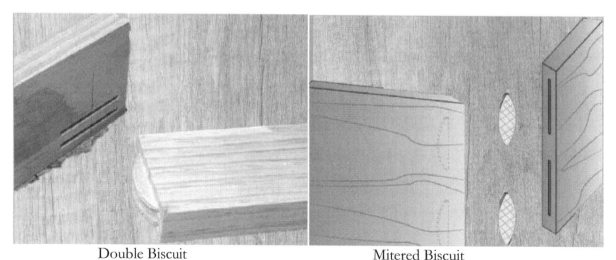
Double Biscuit   Mitered Biscuit

Hold the fence in place, start the saw, and when the electric motor gets to full speed, push the blade into the wood until it doesn't go any further.

After that, withdraw the blade totally and repeat for the following mark.

When all of the ports are ready, apply glue evenly throughout the slots, edge, and place the biscuits.

You'll want to quickly glue each edge of the tabletop and afterward secure the entire piece. Use the clamps to make sure that the entire voids are completely closed. However, be careful to avoid squeezing so hard that the adhesive leaks out.

If any glue does squeeze out of the joints, make sure to wipe it off right away to avoid affecting the surface later on.

8. Pocket Joints

Pocket joints are like a screw that is driven diagonally through one board into another.

Pocket joints are similar to dowel joints and mortise & tenon joints.

For a pocket joint, the course for the screw should be pre-drilled to avoid splitting the head wood. While this can be done in other ways, a much more straightforward approach is using a pocket-hole jig. The screw is driven through the headboard right into the tailwood.

No glue is required, as the screw will hold the joint firmly, but the glue will add more strength to the joint.

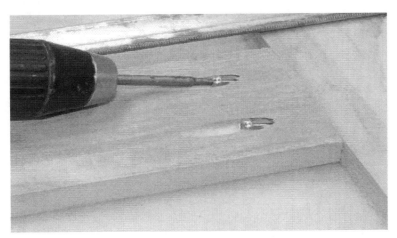

Pocket Joint

Pocket Hole Jigs

Pocket Opening/Hole Jigs:

Improvements in pocket opening jig technology over the last few years have made it easier and more popular.

There are numerous styles of pocket joints, but the major one is a jig with a machined aluminum overview cylinder placed at a specific inclination.

After that, the jig is clamped to the headboard.

A bit that is the same size as the hole and is used to pierce the lightweight aluminum cylinder right into the headboard.

As soon as the pocket opening has been pierced into the headboard, the tailboard is clamped right into the area, and a screw is driven through the pocket opening directly into the tailboard.

If the glue is to be included in strengthening the joint, it needs to be placed on the mating surface area between the tailboard as well as the headboard before putting the screw(s).

Uses of Pocket Joints:

The most popular use for pocket joints is in face frameworks. There are many other possible applications, though. Pocket joints can be used to join sides to make a table or closet top.

They are likewise very efficient in affixing relatively thick edge banding to plywood or a tabletop.

Pocket joints can also be used to attach angled joints in woodworking jobs such as braces for leg rails.

Edge Joint   Example of Pocket Joints

Strength:

Pocket joints are stronger than mortise and tenon joints.

Use

- The pocket joint is mostly used in cabinet frames, face frames, and carcasses.
- Pocket hole joinery makes edging up limited versus tabletops and countertops - and keeps it there.
- Pocket hole joinery provides you with remarkably limited mitered photo framework joints without tough corner-clamping.
- Add extension jamb to a home window or door without visible fasteners. Pocket hole joints keep jambs in place as well as provide a limited, weather-sealed joint.
- Curves - Pocket opening joinery makes it simple to construct odd-angled components and also offers curved forms.

Jamb: A pre-hung door consists of a door hung on hinges and assembled in a **wood frame.

9. Dado Joint

Using a dado is practical and a reliable technique for linking two pieces of wood. When you learn how to cut a dado, you'll choose these woodworking joints that are specifically practical when constructing shelves or cabinet boxes.

This joint is a groove cut into one piece of timber right into which another piece of timber will fit snugly.

For example, when constructing a shelf using 3/4" thick wood, one would cut a 3/4" large groove right into the rack requirement and glue the rack in the slot.

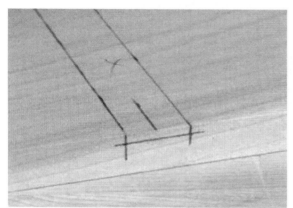

Marking before cutting Dado Joint

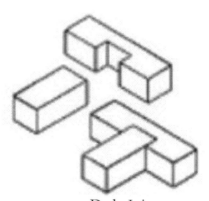

Dado Joint

Techniques for Cutting Dadoes:

There are a couple of techniques for cutting a dado. One of them is to make use of a table saw-based piled dado head cutter.

Broader dadoes can be cut with more than one round through the saw.

A piled dado head cutter collection only needs to be used on a table saw or some radial arm saws.

Do not attempt to make use of a stacked dado head cutting set on a round saw, as this would be exceptionally harmful.

One more option is a "totter" dado set. This is a solitary saw blade set on a flexible spindle. Changing the blade angle on the spindle will change the size of the dado.

While these are much cheaper than a piled dado head cutter set, the results are less reliable.

154

I would certainly resist the urge to purchase a wobble dado and save my money for a high-quality stacked dado collection.

I'm also concerned about safety while using a wobble blade.

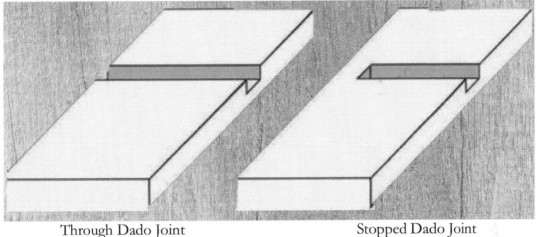

Through Dado Joint   Stopped Dado Joint

Cutting Dadoes with a Router:

Another well-known method for cutting dadoes is to use a straight cutting bit on a router.

When using a router to cut a dado, remember that you'll need to lower the speed quite a bit as well as readjust the deepness for more than one pass to keep from shedding the bit or timber. Use a straight edge to direct the router to guarantee a straight course.

Dado application in table

155

10. Rabbet Joint

A rabbet is like a dado that is cut into the side of the wood face, as opposed to in the center.

A rabbet is suitable for when a rack needs to be positioned back on a cabinet.

How to Cut a Rabbet:

Like a dado, one of the most common ways to cut a rabbet is with a stacked dado head cutting set on a table saw.

Commonly, a sacrificial strip of timber is positioned against the fencing, after which the sacrificial piece is placed against the dado collection.

This method will prevent damage to the table saw's fencing. Another common technique for cutting a rabbet is to use a router table with a straight cutting bit.

Use a feather board to hold the wood down to the table, which will ensure a regular cut.

The rabbet joint is much more powerful than a basic butt joint. It is also conveniently made either with two tables or radial-arm saw cuts (one into the face, the second right into the edge or end grain) or with one pass through a saw outfitted with a dado head.

The rabbet joint is used to establish backboards onto the rear of a case piece or to accommodate the glass on a mirror frame.

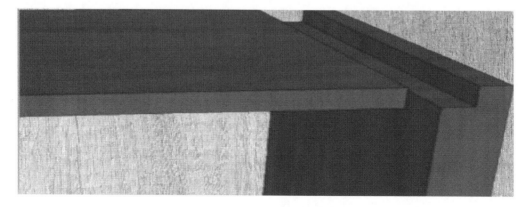

Basic Rabbet Joint

Dual Rabbet

The dual rabbet joint has a rabbet cut in both mating pieces. This joint is more durable than the basic rabbet for several reasons.

Rabbet and Dual Rabbet

The second rabbet supplies an extra gluing area to the joint as well as the additional ninety-degree shoulder.

Careful measurement, as well as cutting, is needed to make the joint fit without voids when cutting by hand.

They are made much more precisely on either a table saw or a router table.

This is an outstanding joint for the top corners of high bookcases as well as cupboards that won't be fitted with a face framework. The joint can be additionally boosted with equally spaced dowels driven in from the side.

Mitered Rabbet

The mitered rabbet might look challenging, yet with an excellent table saw or router table, it's not so bad. Once the equipment is appropriately set up, any kind of variety of these joints can be done quickly.

157

A mitered rabbet is probably one of the most attractive of all the variations of the rabbet joint.

It effectively hides completion grain and gives the joint a beautiful mitered appearance. You'll find this joint in luxury closets and cabinet boxes.

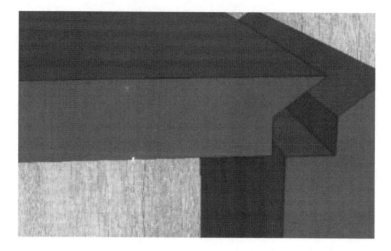

Mitered Rabbet

11. Dovetail Joints

a) Through Dovetail Joint

Dovetail is prized not only for its strength but also for its looks.

Dovetail joints can be tricky to style. However, dovetailing jigs and routers have made this joint much easier to perfect.

The dovetail joint is most commonly used in drawer building and construction.

However, there are several other kinds of joints that might be better suited to specific scenarios.

For instance, half-blind dovetails are used when the sides of the drawer need to connect straight with the face of the drawer.

Dovetails on cabinets should only be visible when the drawer is opened.

Blind dovetails are common in closet or box building and construction where the pins and tails must be wholly concealed.

Nevertheless, a section of the end grain of the tail wood will certainly be visible.

If the woodworker wants to hide the pins, tails as well as end grains, a mitered dovetail is the very best choice. Nonetheless, this is a complex joint, which takes a reasonable amount of time and patience to master.

There are numerous other variants on the classic dovetail, including rabbet through dovetails, mitered through dovetails, beveled dovetails, and box joints (which are essential dovetails with rectangle-shaped pins and tails).

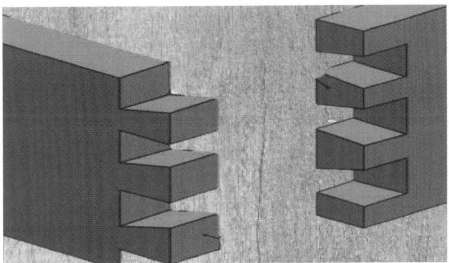

Through Dovetail Joint

Typical Creation of Through Dovetails:

Before the development of dovetailing jigs, dovetails were cut by hand, and some woodworkers today still choose this traditional technique.

The actions are fairly basic:

1. Plane the ends of the two pieces of wood in a wood square.

2. Mark the shoulder line of each piece, equal to the size of the adjacent piece.

3. Mark the ends of the tails at the desired angle.

4. Cut the tails with a dovetailing saw.

5. Remove the excess between the tails.

159

6. Utilizing the finished tails, note the pins on the contrary board.

7. Cut the pins and clean the waste.

Evaluate the joint's fit and cut more off the pins if required.

Utilizing a Dovetailing Jig:

To make a hole in dovetails with a dovetailing jig, the order is essentially the same. Mark the depth of the cut on the tailboard and insert it right into the jig.

Mount an appropriate dovetailing bit right into your router and cut the tails. Next, following the jig's directions, insert the pinboard into the jig in the proper location, switch to a straight cutting bit, and cut the pins.

Undoubtedly, the details for this procedure depend on the picked jig. Nonetheless, each dovetailing system includes a full, step-by-step set of instructions for cutting through dovetails.

Setting up:

Dovetails should fit snugly, but not be too tight. Consistently dry-fit your dovetails before you get to the last step, to guarantee your joint is perfect.

When dry-fitting through dovetails, they need to be a bit hard to take apart, but not so tough that you need a mallet to divide the parts.

When constructing through dovetails, spread a thin layer of woodworking glue on all surfaces of either the tails or the pins before placing the joint together.

Use a rubber club or a sacrificial block of timber with a claw hammer to stay clear of ruining the joint. Immediately wipe away any kind of extra glue.

The Secret to Perfect Dovetails:

If there is one rule to follow, no matter which technique you choose to cut your dovetails, it is this: **always cut the tails first, then cut the pins to fit the tails.**

It is much easier to take a bit more off the pins to make sure they fit the tails. Nonetheless, if you cut the pins first, the tails are far tougher to mark, increasing the probability of an incomplete dovetail joint.

b) Half-Blind Dovetail Joint

When connecting two pieces of wood, possibly the most prominent joint is the through dovetail.

The through dovetails are solid and look good. However, there are circumstances where it is not the right choice.

Like when connecting sides of a drawer directly to the drawer front, the ends of the tails will show in the drawer front if through dovetail is used.

In this case, the best sort of dovetail joint to use is the half-blind dovetail

Half Dovetail Joint

What is a Half-Blind Dovetail?

The half-blind dovetail is as precise as the name implies, i.e., only half of the joint is visible. This joint is almost as solid as the through dovetail but is used in scenarios such as the cabinet front situation outlined above.

Standard steps for cutting half-blind dovetails:

1. Plane the ends of both pieces of a wood square.

2. Mark the size of the tails, which is the size of the pinboard minus the lap. Make a shoulder line of the appropriate size around the tailboard.

3. Mark the tails at the preferred angle.

4. Cut the tails with a dovetailing saw.

5. Remove the waste between the tails using a bevel-edged chisel.

6. Using the finished tails, note the pins on the pinboard, lining up the shoulder cuts with the side of the pinboard opposite the lap.

7. Cut the pins and clean the waste using a chisel.

Joint only visible on the inside

Utilizing a Dovetailing Jig:

While almost all router-based dovetail jigs can puncture dovetails, only some specific methods can cut half-blind dovetails. Keep this in mind when buying a dovetail jig system for your store.

The treatment for cutting half-blind dovetails with a dovetail jig system is the same standard treatment. Mark the deepness of the cut on the tailboard based upon the size of the pinboard minus the lap.

Insert the tailboard right into the jig and cut the tails utilizing a suitable dovetailing router bit. Then, following the jig's guidelines, mark and cut the half-blind pins in the pinboard.

b) Sliding Dovetail Joint

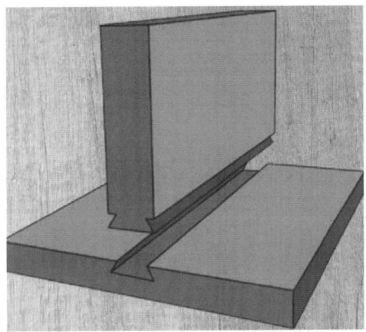

Sliding Dovetail Joint

Of all dovetail joints, the sliding dovetail might be the least well-known, particularly among woodworking beginners.

However, the sliding dovetail might be the most versatile of all dovetail joints.

It's not only handy for attaching two pieces of wood at a right-angle. It is also used to connect parts together in closet doors or cutting boards, for attaching table legs to stands and joining racks to cabinet instances.

This joint is made by cutting a single tail down the size of a board's side, which is slid right into a matching pin-shaped slot in the receiving item of wood. It is better to taper the slot in the receiving piece somewhat, to ensure that the joint is tighter towards the rear.

It will make the joint much more comfortable to slide in. It will also assist in maintaining the joint from splitting apart in the future.

Cutting a Sliding Dovetail Joint:

Typically, a sliding dovetail was made by cutting the tail and slotting it by hand and cleaning up the parts with a chisel.

Nevertheless, some modern-day dovetail jigs have the option to cut sliding dovetails with a router and a dovetail bit.

While this might remove some of the mystique of the joint, it makes the job a lot easier to do over and over, along with being a lot quicker.

If you have a dovetail jig that can cut a sliding dovetail joint, the actions for doing so need to be spelled out in the customer overview that comes with the dovetail jig.

12. Box Joint

The dovetail joint is a timeless, stunning & reliable method for attaching two pieces of wood. However, the dovetail joint can't be used in all cases.

For example, what if you need to attach two pieces of plywood?

Making use of dovetails to attach plywood would considerably boost the chances of peeling the plywood when examining the joint while dry fitting.

Box Joint

What happens if you do not have access to a dovetail jig and router?

This is if you don't want to go to the trouble of hand-sewing dovetails. Is there another alternative apart from dovetails to use in your woodworking tasks?

A simple alternative to the dovetail is the box joint.

As you can see, a box joint is similar to a dovetail, with the distinction of the rectangular fingers.

Naturally, you could always do it with a dovetail saw and a chisel. Choose a width for the fingers that will divide evenly right into the wood width.

If your wood is 6 inches wide, a half-inch finger will permit twelve fingers overall, six on each piece of wood.

The glued box joint has a high glued surface leading to a strong bond that is similar to a finger joint. Box joints are used for edges of boxes or box-like constructions, hence the name.

13. Bridle Joint

Bridle joints are similar to mortise and tenon joints.

The difference is in the dimension of the mortise and tenon. As these joints still have a mortise and tenon, they are durable and look appealing.

165

The distinction in the bridle joints and mortise and tenon stays in the size of the tenon and deepness of the mortise.

The tenon on this joint is as long as the deepness of the hardwood.

This allows both wood pieces to lock tightly. The new area allows the opportunity to add more glue, which makes it more robust.

These are popular joints for joining rails, legs, and stiles.

Bridle Joint Pros

- A less complicated option to the mortise and tenon joint
- Can shape joint set up without giving up on strength
- Great for creating slim frameworks
- One of the essential joints to cut
- Does not need mortising equipment

Bridle Joint Cons
- Can see the end grain

Types of Bridle Joint

Corner Bridle Joints can be used as a more comfortable replacement for a haunched mortise and tenon joint, especially where the structure is to be skinned or covered (e.g., frames for loose, cushioned chair seats).

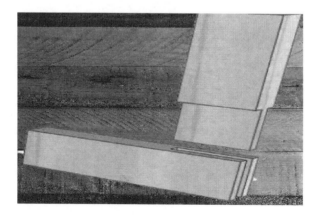

Corner Bridle

166

Tee Bridle Joints can be used as an easier option to a mortise as well as a tenon joint, but where a harder joint is required.

Tee Bridle

Mitered Corner Bridle Joints are used where a tougher joint than a mitered halving joint is required and where a molding, groove, or refund runs round the edge (e.g., mirror structures). Either or both sides of the outlet may be mitered as required.

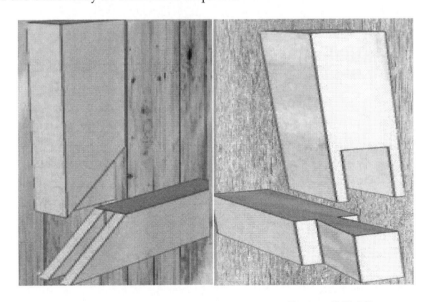

Mitered Bridle   Dovetail Bridle

167

Dovetailed Bridle joints can be used where there is some propensity for the joint to be pulled apart.

14. Dowel Joint

Dowel joints are the most durable joint type when it comes to woodworking, especially when utilizing numerous rows of dowels. Dowels develop strong joints that are easy to create in your home. This joint is used for building reliable, accurate joints in timber.

Two Dowel Joint

They are thicker and more durable than nails or screws, and for that reason, they are much less susceptible to breaking.

They provide a stronger joint than just using adhesive.

This joint is pretty self-explanatory. As one of the many variations of a butt joint, the dowel joint is one of the most prominent joints.

It is used to make tabletops, cupboards, and chairs, to name a few. Dowel joints give the impression of a conventional butt joint.

The dowel joint uses round 'pins' (the dowels mentioned above) to hold the joint together.

These sorts of joints call for careful preparation and the adhesive to be as strong as possible.

You have to pierce two aligning holes that are half the depth of the dowel itself. You use adhesive in the holes to keep the dowel in nice and tight!

Dowels kept for use

Gradually the adhesive, naturally, can dry out.

Nonetheless, the advantage of a dowel joint is that typically the dowels will keep your piece together.

This creaking and contraction of the timber is one reason why dowel joints are not frequently used in higher-end hand-made furniture.

Box with Dowel Joint

Dowel Joint Pros

- Dowling is a quick process.
- It helps to ensure a smooth finish.
- Screws, nails, or other tools are not needed.
- Dowel joints are the strongest kinds of joints in woodworking, especially when using multiple rows of dowels.
- Dowels assist in producing solid joints that are easy to make in your home.

Dowel Joint Cons

- Misalignment of Joints
- Dowel Shearing
- No Face to Face Grain Union

15. Finger Joint

As per Wikipedia: *A finger joint is also called a comb joint; it is a woodworking joint made by cutting a collection of corresponding interlocking accounts in two kinds of wood, which are then glued. The cross-section of the joint resembles the interlocking of fingers between 2 hands; for this reason, the name "finger joint."*

A conical or scarfed finger joint is one of the most common joints used to create long lumber pieces from strong boards. The result is finger-jointed lumber. The finger joint can also be useful when creating walls, molding or trim, and can also be used in floorboards and door building.

Finger joints allow for more robust parts while considerably reducing waste (which saves money in the long run). The benefits of finger-jointed lumber are straightness and dimensional stability.

Finger Joints are used for various projects like:

- Board Door Frame
- Flooring
- Boxes

There are many variations of finger joints, such as :

Square finger joint

Stepped finger joint

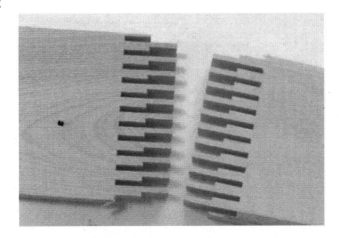

Slanted cut finger joint

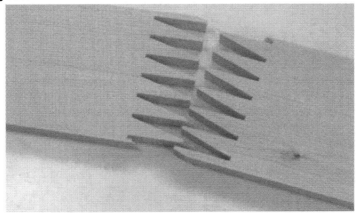

Finger Joint Pros

- Makes a straighter joint
- Much less timber is wasted
- Budget-friendly
- Resilient for an upright load
- Adhesives can be applied, allowing a more robust joint than mortise and tenon

Finger Joint Cons

- Can appear misaligned
- Harder to get a smooth wall

5. Japanese Joinery

Introduction

Unlike many traditional joinery techniques, Japanese joinery has until recently remained a closelipped craft among carpentry family members in Japan.

The detailed joints are made with precision and ability, making use of various end, corner, and intermediate joints to thoroughly counteract tons and torsions.

These have parts set up like puzzles to develop smart structures, which are understood to be among several of the oldest surviving structures today.

As opposed to the basic types of timber building, Japanese joinery doesn't depend on irreversible fixtures such as screws, nails, and adhesives. Instead, joints are securely safeguarded with interlocking connections.

Due to 3D visualizations, the intricacies behind these have been disclosed to crafters and manufacturers alike, offering the possibility to re-establish Japanese joinery into buildings.

Traditional Japanese Joinery

173

Centuries before the development of screws and fasteners, Japanese artisans used complex, interlacing joints to attach pieces of timber. I know it might be a bit more time consuming; however, I have started using Japanese joints to construct my recent furnishings. Using less hardware is a clear advantage.

Japanese carpenters can tell you a lot regarding a wood's quality and its suitability for a project.

Experienced woodworkers can differentiate between root and branch end, which helps in deciding where to divide the wood piece.

Also, they understand the type of timber through appearance, feel, and also odor, as well as how the timber was dried.

Many people don't demonstrate the skill they have. Japanese carpenters show their skill: the keshōmen, or "decorative face" of a piece of wood.

The distinct arch pattern you usually see on the face of a board is the result of "simple sawing." Ordinary sawing is one of the most efficient ways to cut a log, leaving the facility core to be used for columns. Yet, carpenters consider it to be the least sophisticated way for the timber.

The pattern is quite attractive, and plain-sawn lumber wastes extremely little wood, but the "arcs" that show up on the lumber's face also mean that it is somewhat weaker than a piece where the grain is vertical. Sometimes those arcs will split from the cut plane.

Additionally, an imperfect reducing blade may catch on the development rings and gash the wood.

Plain-sawn lumber tends to shrink more as it dries out, and may additionally "mug," its face becoming concave.

Due to this, Japanese woodworkers are specific concerning which side of a piece of lumber is the crucial face - the keshōmen to be displayed in the completed work - and which is inconsequential. When they make use of a plain-sawn board, the face displaying the grain's arches will always be dominant - but the unsightly end needs to be covered.

A great woodworker can tell whether the board is likely to cup, and will also ensure weak boards are not used where they will be seen.

Better Cuts for Stunning Grain

Quartersawn timber decreases the likelihood of issues of cupping, shrinkage, and splitting. However, this technique of cutting even more of the timber is a lot more work, making it extra pricey.

Nevertheless, every surface area of the board can conveniently be used as a keshōmen.

**Quartersawn lumber is the angle that the annular growth rings intersect the face of the board.

Types of Japanese Joints

- **Interlocking Tenon Joint:** Used for making a staircase or chair. Two or more pieces are attached.

- **Interlocking miter joint:** It's a half=lap type joint used in heavy frame construction.

- **Threeway corner miter joint:** Three pieces have miter here, with a leg feature as tenon, which fits with the other two pieces as shown below.

- **Three-way pinned corner miter joint:** This joint is similar to the earlier one but has an additional pin, as shown below.

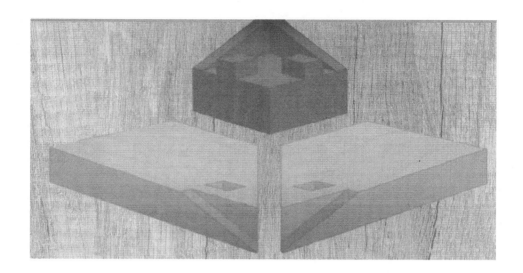

- **Secret mitered dovetail joints**

  Also called full blind mitered joints, these joints are strong and suitable for cabinet and box works.

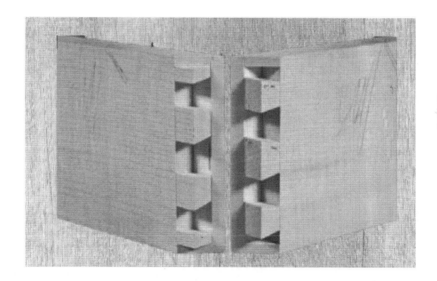

- **Shelf assistance joint:** This joint is used for cases where a heavy load is required to be held on the shelf. Dado shelf is used at the end of the shelf to support the load.

- **Divided mortise and tenon joint:**

Tenons cut into rails mesh together. These are used in large panels and frames.

- **Mitered shoulder tenon joint:** Similar to the last joint with one side of the mortise and tenon beveled as shown.

- **Sliding dovetail joint:** Used in chair construction to connect legs to the rail.

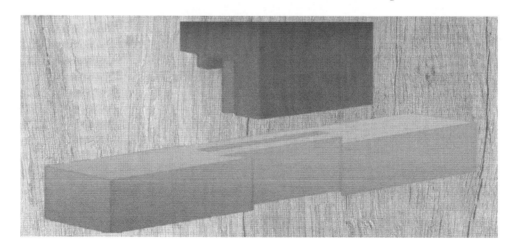

- **Mitered corner joint:** This joint is used predominantly in large structures/frames.

6. CNC Wood Joinery

Joinery is a part of woodworking that includes joining pieces of wood to create more complex products. Some timber joints utilize fasteners, bindings, or adhesives, while others use just wood aspects. The qualities of wooden joints like strength, adaptability, toughness, and appearance stem from the properties of the joining products and how they are used in the joints.

CNC Joints

CNC joinery differs from conventional woodworking joints. Round interior edges can create uncomfortable and even unpleasant joints. However, the ability to reproduce specific activities makes these joints a breeze.

Tolerance

The secret to good joinery is identifying the correct amount of tolerance.

"Tolerance describes the max error one can endure; according to the practical precision, one can anticipate from himself. Each people must establish his/her tolerance."

Considerations in CNC Cut Joinery

Below are the few factors to consider for CNC joinery.

Devices:

Instead of router bits, saw blades are used.

Wear and tear on the edge of the wood is much more problematic with router bits.

It requires meticulous setup, so the device works correctly.

Router bits exert more pressure on the workpiece while cutting and requiring stronger fixturing.

Routing plywood shape cuts are usually machined with a compression bit. This bit is lowered from the top as well as raised from the bottom to minimize tear in sheet woods.

Pockets are generally cut with down shear bits to reduce tear-out.

Corners:

Square corners can't be cut with cylindrical router bits. In several scenarios, this indicates joints need to be made with rounded corners.

The rounded corners can be pierced or routed.

 A crucial point with routing these corners is that the tool must keep being moved while making the cut. Otherwise, extreme heat develops.

This will wear down the tool and create the risk of fire.

Tolerance:

Two mating parts won't fit together if cut the same size.

A void needs to exist between the parts for them to slide into one another as well as for adhesive.

 In CNC, it's common to use a void of 0.005" per side of the joint. So, for instance, a tenon needs to be cut 2 times 0.005" narrower than the mortise (0.005" on each side). This is a rather limited fit yet will certainly work if the maker is accurate, and the tools are sharp.

If the devices are plain, then the cut will not be as tidy, and the precision can't be kept. Therefore, it is sometimes necessary to use 0.01" per side.

Wood:

Product thickness variants have a huge influence on the digital joints.

 For a specific thickness, tool path programming will be done.

If the wood is not that specific density, it will affect the fit of the joint.

Because of this, "Wood to leave" and also "Flooring to leave" parameters in the CAM software program can offer offsets to make up for the variation.

Fixturing:

Rather than moving the job piece over the device, the job must be held firmly while the tool moves.

The procedure for safeguarding the work is called fixturing.

When it comes to 3-axis routing of plywood, this indicates tabbing the components. For hardwood, this typically involves double-sided tape holding the components to a spoil board.

CNC Cut Joint Examples:

There are several exciting joints that can be quickly cut on the CNC, which would be very time-consuming if made with standard shop tools.

Types of CNC joints:

3-Axis CNC Corner Joints
These joints affix members along an edge to create an edge, in 3-axis joinery, generally at 90 degrees.

- **Finger Tenons**
These are one of the simplest CNC joints which are exposed at the corner. Sufficient surface is available for glue.

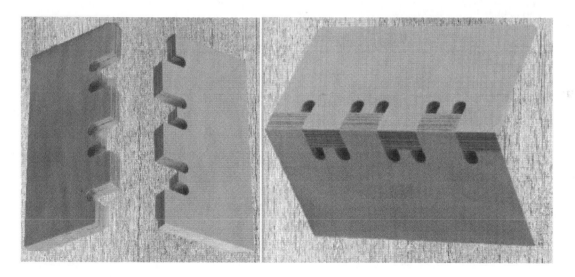

- **Blind Finger Tenons**
This uses pockets along the edge of the joint to stop the tenons from showing through. This is described as a blind joint. The sides are visible from the outside.

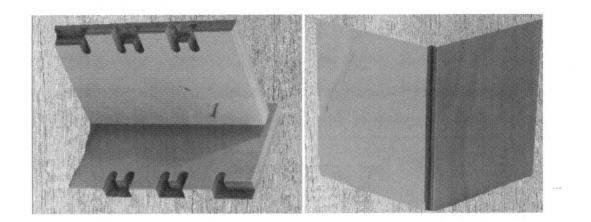

- **Lapped Fingertip Tenons**

This is a type of half-blind joint. It is made by cutting pockets for all the fingers to slot right into one side only.

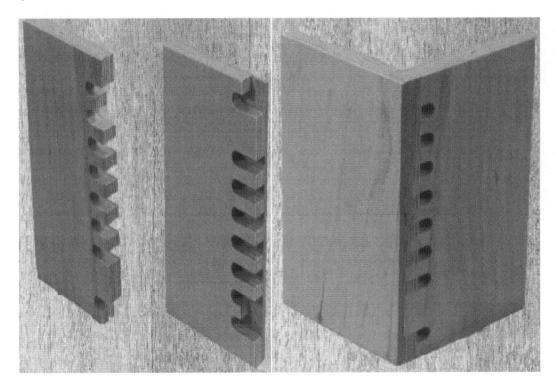

- **Fingertip Tenons**

The two parts are identical. They give a lot of adhesive areas and allow a stable connection. Here, the narrower tenons are referred to as "fingertip" as opposed to "finger."

184

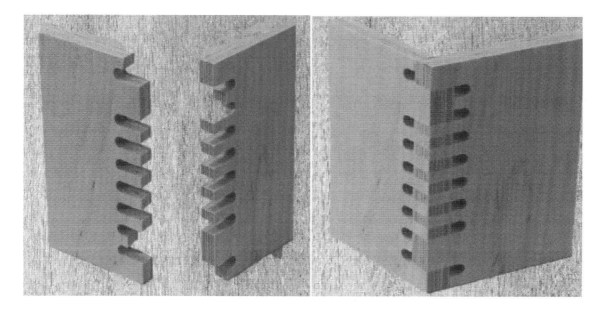

- **Hammer Tenons**

This joint is made to keep the joint from pulling apart along one axis mechanically. You can see precisely how the fingers lock over the grooves in the mating fingers' edges. The name comes from the hammerhead form on the right. Some joints are created to break down or split conveniently.

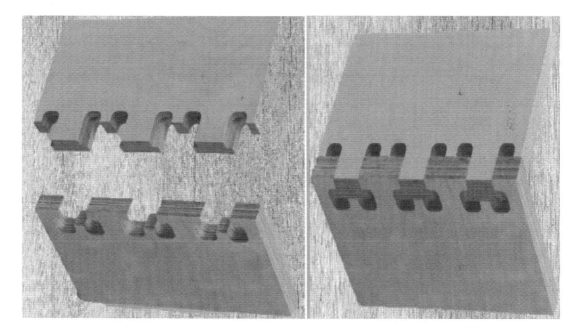

- **Fingertip Tenons along with key**

The lengthened tenons of this joint have a notch that accepts a key that protects the joint from tension.

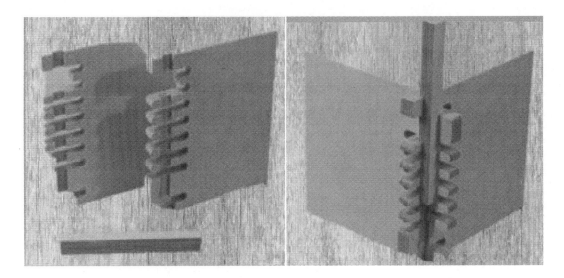

Right here, it partly removed, revealing the grooves in each wood.

- **Catch Tenon**

This is a type of break-down joint. The components are slid into each other, and the catch is pressed via the matching lock. The tenon flips down and hooks to protect the joint from splitting through stress.

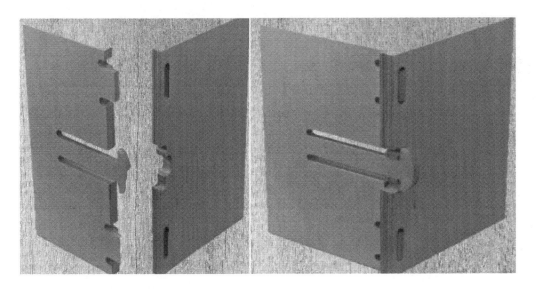

The catch is pocked to the half-thickness to make it much easier to flex over the latch.

- **Doweled mortise and through tenon**

This example uses a dowel to prevent one part from sliding back through the other. When the dowel is tight versus the face of the mating wood, the joint is rather solid. Note that the joint above uses a drill to get rid of the edge product. Earlier joints used the router a bit. This decision has a significant effect on the look of the joint.

3-Axis CNC Housing Joints
These joints attach two parts in a perpendicular manner.

- **Through Finger Tenons**

This is an example of a through the joint where the tenons of the vertical participant show through the side.

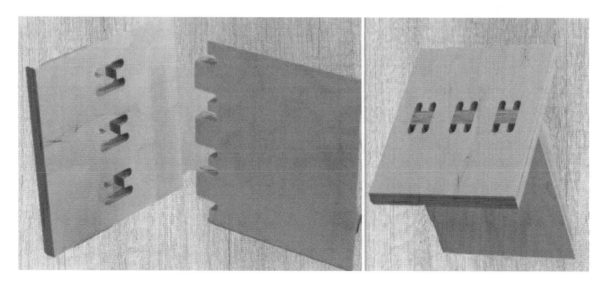

- **Through Fingertip Tenons**

This joint provides a greater surface area for the glue. Refer to the below picture:

- **Clip Tenons**

The long tenons flex just enough to allow them to get right into the mortises. When fully through, they hook over and below the mortises to lock them into place.

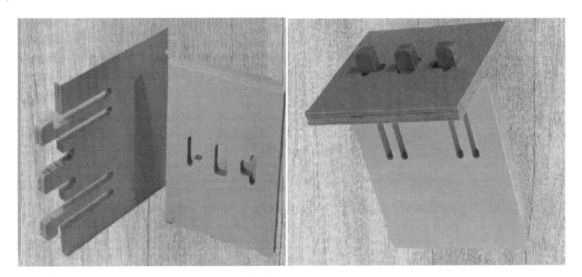

3-Axis CNC Structure Joints

These structure joints enable components to attach in a T or X arrangement. They are typically half-laps. That is, the product is removed from both pieces to permit them to overlap. Normally the product is removed midway through each piece.

- **Oval Shouldered Halving**

Basic curved edge half-lap joint. The components are identical. This joint is decoratively contrasted to a regular half-lap but is still steady. The curves give some extra tensile strength as well as a boosted glue area alongside the joint. In all half-lap joints, the product thickness is vital to a precise fit.

- **Dovetailed Cross Halving**

This joint has two of the same components. They provide a high level of racking resistance and a lot of glue area.

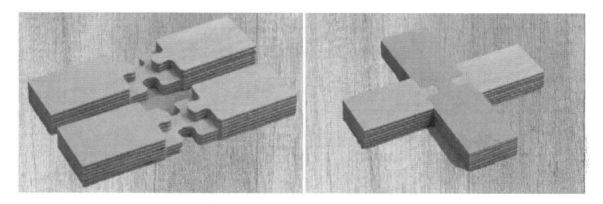

- **Jigsaw Cross Halving**

A joint is similar to the one over, although these parts are mirror images of one another.

- **Cross Miter Joint with Jigsaw Key**

This joint enables four different pieces to join up with an intersection area, making use of a jigsaw key. In a suitable tight joint, this is extremely challenging to take apart. In a joint loosened sufficiently where the joint can be easily uncoupled, the holding of the four members is not really inflexible.

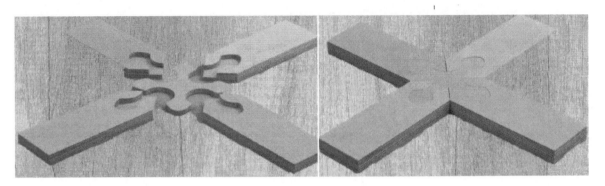

The adhering of joints is done at a T junction instead of an X.

- **Stop Lap with Jigsaw Key**

This jigsaw essential offers some stress resistance. This joint additionally has a notch cut in the side so the cross participant can withstand lateral anxieties too.

- **Jigsaw Miter Joint**

An additional decorative half-lap corner joint that offers resistance to riving because of the interlocking components.

- **Miter Joint with Butterfly Key**

A butterfly key is used to hold the two pieces together. The thickness of the key is half the density of the material.

3-Axis CNC Edge-To-Edge Joints

These joints join two wood pieces end to finish or edge to edge.

Lapped Dovetail

This joint allows two boards to be connected along their edges. It has a beautiful decorative effect, and the dovetail form offers mechanical resistance against pulling apart. At the rear end of the joint, the edge is a straight line.

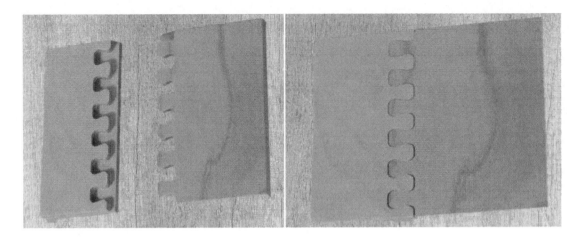

Dual Lapped Dovetail

Double dovetails are a variation. So the ornamental tails show up on each side of the wood.

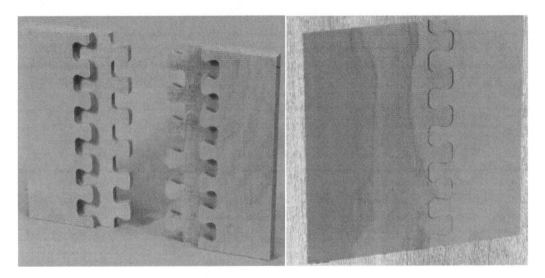

Board Extending with Jigsaw Keys

These joints use removable keys to join edges with the boards.

These keys are tough to get in as well as out of the pockets if the fit is excellent. So these are not suitable as knock-down (uncouple) joints.

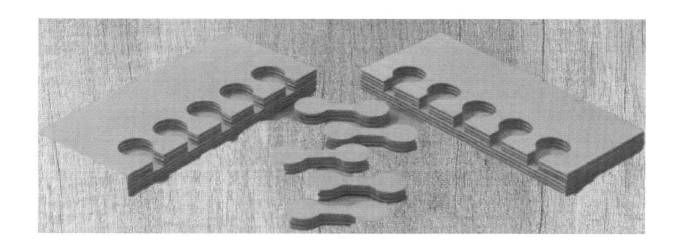

Board Lengthening with Unbalanced Dovetail Keys

This is a joint that uses more commonly shaped dovetails. Butterfly keys resemble this although they are in proportion regarding their centerline (these are crooked).

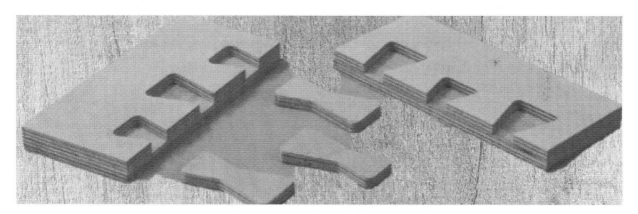

Ginkgo Scarf with Stub Tenons

The form of this joint echoes the Ginko tree leaf and also demonstrates the convenience with which the CNC can cut complicated contours.

Gooseneck Mortise as well as Tenon Joint with Stub Tenons
Same principle as above – various types of geometry to this variation.

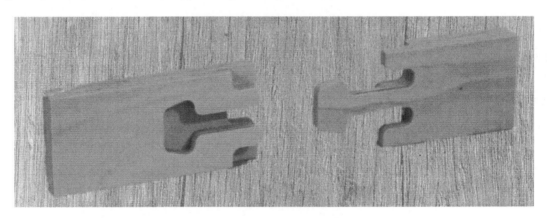

Dual Jigsaw
Both parts of this joint style are comparable but are mirror images of each other.

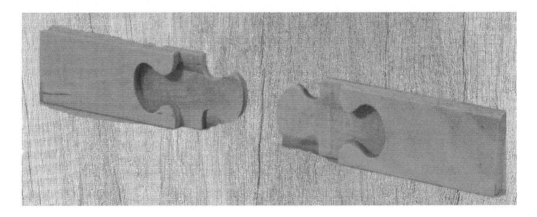

Halving with Elliptical Machine Tenon

This joint is used where the two parts are each thinned by one-half and overlap each other. The ellipse tenon in this joint provides mechanical resistance to pulling apart. This joint would be weak in wood because the sheer plane is alongside the wood fibers (so-called short-grain).

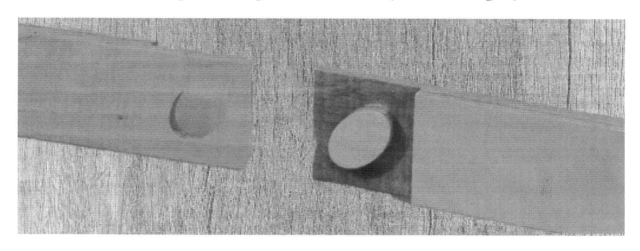

Triple Dovetail

Single dovetail on one side, double on the other. Unlike the joint over, these are not aligned side to side, making it stronger.

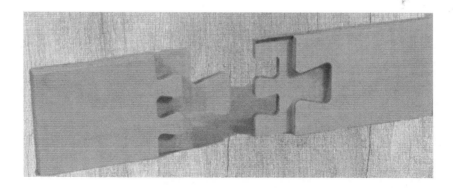

7. Joinery Projects for Beginners

1. Table Leg Assembly Using Mortise and Tenon Joinery

Materials:

- Wood board
- Wood glue
- Parallel clamps
- Spiral feather board
- Rubber mallet
- Table saw

One of the most basic joinery methods is mortise and tenon. This is a fantastic joint for table legs, and with a few tools, it can be very strong.

Milling and Marking

The first step is to get your wood and material for the project.

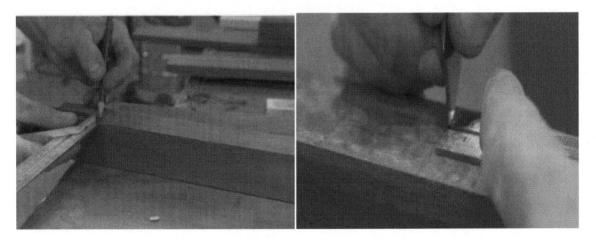

The more the wood is shaped and squared, the better for the project. If the timber is only recently dried, leave a day between each milling step.

This will allow the timber to move as the stress is released.

As soon as the wood is cut square and is sized, it's time to mark it out for the mortise, the holes in the legs.

In this situation, the rail will be the tenon, so all the rails must be of the same dimension.

A lot of hardwoods splinter quickly, so breaking the timber fibers along the line implies you'll have cleaner lines.

Use a combination square mark on the front-facing edge. Make this the same right around the table on each leg.

This line will be cut initially because it's what individuals will see, any modifications will be made on the line facing inwards.

The next step is to draw the line on the other side to represent the rail width. Then cut along the lines using a marking knife.

Eliminating Material from the Leg

After marking out the leg, we require the removal of the product.

Use a drill press to eliminate most of it. However, the router needs to be under as little stress as possible to guarantee a clean cut.

Drill a series of openings making use of a depth quit, leaving several millimeters before the line.

Now set up a stop block for the router, so you don't mistakenly cut too far, and begin getting rid of along the cut line.

Setup the fence on the router, so you're cutting on the line of the outdoor face of the rail/leg.

Do all the legs with this setting on the fencing, so they're the same.

Beware cutting in both directions as the router will react in a different way to the feed direction.

This highlights the need to get rid of as much wood as possible using the drill press.

As soon as you've done all the legs with the fence one established, move to cut along the various other lines and repeat.

At this stage, the rails need to either be a tight fit or not be able to fit.

I prefer to cut the mortises undersize as well as sand the rails to fit. Cutting the mortise too large is not recommended.

Cut Rail

Cut the mortise into the leg to be smaller than the height of the rail.

Make a small notch out of the bottom of the rail in each edge, enough to ensure that the edge rests against the leg.

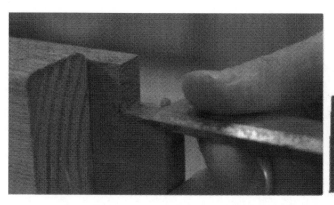 

The sharper this cut is, the far better it will look. Use a marking knife to cut all the lines.

Glue

As you have a tight fit, you can glue the parts together.

Use clamps to draw the legs right into the rail.

You can improve with lots of practice and by not repeating mistakes.

2. Small Table with Pocket Hole Joinery

Materials:

- A pocket hole jig set
- Pocket screws drill and driver bar clamps
- (4) tapered legs 1 3/4" square by 10" tall (any size will do depending on your need)
- Some scrap birch or other wood for the stool skirt and saw of choice
- Stain and finish safety glasses

Getting the pieces all set

Initially tear up some scrap birch to 3" broad.

After that, cut two wood pieces 15 1/2" long for the sides as well as two pieces 8 1/4" for the ends.

Use the pocket opening jig to position screw holes on the top and end edges.

The screw holes will be within the constructed stool so they won't show.

Assembly

Make one side at a time.

Put glue on each end of an end piece.

Keep two legs upside down and clamp them to the center of the end piece.

The primary factor in using a clamp is that pocket screws will push away from the target timber sometimes and won't screw in straight.

After you insert the screws, you won't need the clamp any longer. Repeat the action on the opposite side.

Join both ends to both sides once more using a clamp.

Go easy with the adhesive. If adhesive spurts out, clean it up with a damp cloth quickly.

Adding a Top

Cut another piece of wood 11 1/2" by 19" to be the top.

It might fit as a top for your stool.

Run a grain of glue around the top of your stool. Center your stool and screw it to the top.

Sand the surface.

Stain and Finish

Use your selection of stain, preferably two layers.

For example, you can use excellent old Minwax tarnish, and leave it to completely dry.

The benefit of water-based finishes is that they dry out quickly. You can use three coats of water-based semi-gloss poly.

202

The stool was built-in around an hour approximately. Finishing would not take long. You have to wait a while between layers.

3. Box using Box Joint

Materials:

3-4" wide board

Scrap board

Router table and a 1/4" straight bit

Compound miter saw, or table saw

Planer/Joiner

Belt sander

Straight file

Some clamps

Prepare the sides

Plane your board to the preferred thickness. I used a 2.5" broad maple planed to 3/8" thickness.

Cut four sides. Tag each wood piece lightly with a pencil: front, back, left, and right—this aids in putting the tag at the top of each wood piece for positioning later.

Prepare the jig

For this box, I wanted 1/4" fingers. I placed a 1/4" straight bit into the router table and also set the height to be the thickness of my sides. A quick method to do this is to stack two wood pieces on top of each other with one offset from the other. Raise the router bit until it simply touches the offset wood on top. Do not change the height.

Take a piece of scrap wood and clamp it to your miter scale. In my situation, I required an added piece of scrap to provide an excellent securing surface on the back of the miter gauge. The front piece is flush with the surface of the router table; the 2nd clamping piece removes the router a little bit.

Turn on the router and rout a rectangle-shaped hole in the front piece of scrap. This hole will hold the jig "finger."

Cut a piece of wood, probably from your board, just a bit larger than your bit size, in my case 1/4" x 1/4" x ~ 2".

Fit the piece into the slot you cut in the jig board. File or sand it to a tight fit. Additionally, sand the bottom down.

Currently, realign the jig board on the router table, against the miter gauge. This time, however, you will secure the board offset from the bit by the width of the bit(1/4"). I used a 1/4" drill bit as a spacer in between the jig finger and the little router bit.

Clamp the jig board into place. Be sure you are gauging against the widest part of the router bit and that the fit is as specific as you can get. This action determines precisely how well the box will fit.

Cut the fingers on the first wood.

Now, you can start cutting the fingers. It is an excellent idea to do some test fingers on a couple of scrap wood pieces to evaluate the positioning of the jig. If the fingers don't fit very tightly, try the placement once again.

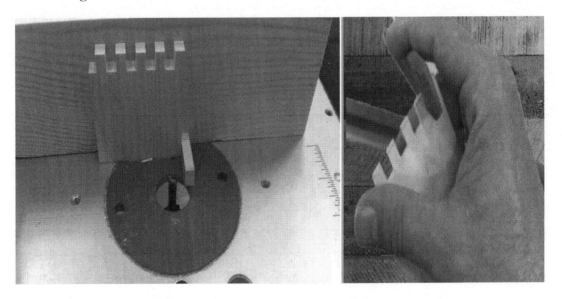

For the first cut: Straighten one side of the side wood with the inside side of the jig finger. Make a hole. You need a piece with a 1/4" square hole, 1/4" in from the left side.

For the second and following cuts: move the piece to ensure that the slot you cut fits over the jig finger. Create a brand-new hole. Repeat until you run out of the board. If the last hole doesn't straighten flawlessly with the side, do not worry, the corresponding piece will have the exact same quantity of leftover hole.

In between creating holes, mainly if the jig finger is a limited fit, you might want to run a square data with the newly reduced hole to change the fit. Don't file away too much, just enough for it to fit securely.

Cut the fingers on the second wood piece.
The second piece of wood is cut like the first one.

Evaluate your fit
Dry fit your wood. If it is too tight, attempt some light filing, if it is also loose, attempt once again with a much better dimension on the jig finger and the router bit placement.

Make the other two sides
Cut fingers on all eight sides, adhering to the same rules as the first two sides.

Bottom and Cover

For this box, I wanted a cover that would fit freely into the top and bottom. The miter gauge would help to keep the lid square when routing the short side.

Glue and finish

My box joint fingers were so tight that I had to use a club. The bottom wood glued in quickly, and the lid fits well at the top. Use stain or repaint as you want.

4. Chisel Box Using Japanese Joinery

Materials Required:

- Scrap Wood (If available, I recommend wood-paulownia wood)
- Chisel
- Hand Saw
- Planar
- Pencil

- Take out pieces of scrap wood and clean it of their coating and then shape them.
- The box has six sides, so pick two broader pieces for the base and lid and the leftover four for sides.
- Keep the largest chisel on the base and make lines for cutting in the shape of Japanese joinery, as shown below.

209

- Cut the mortise and tenon, as shown by the pencil in the base and side wood pieces.
- Measure the side joint as per the tenon in the base joint, as shown below. Carve out the tenon in the side wood piece as per this measurement.

- Carve out similar tenon and mortise respectively on the other end of the wood pieces.
- Make similar length and breadth pieces of the box with similar mortise and tenon measurements.
- Run a dry fit, as shown in the below picture. (Without lid)

- Carve out the lid as per the measurement of the base wood piece.
- Cover the box with the lid.
- Go ahead with the finishing and coloring as per your choice.

5. Bench

Material Required

- Wood Piece (You need 2 leg,1 leg joiner, and 1 lid piece)
- Smoothing Plane
- Table Saw
- Marking Gauge
- Hand Saw
- Driller
- Chisel
- Marking Knife
- Sander

- Break down the wood and do the milling process to make the wood flat, square, and smooth.
- Alternatively you can buy S4S lumber (already milled on four sides).

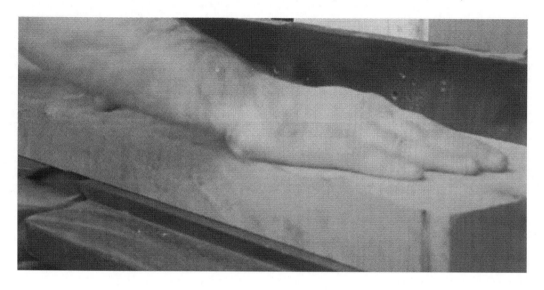

- Apply glue to the two boards, as shown below.
- Use the clamp and apply pressure to stick them.

- After the glue has dried, pass the joined plank through the thickness planar. Then apply a smoothing plane to all the wood pieces.

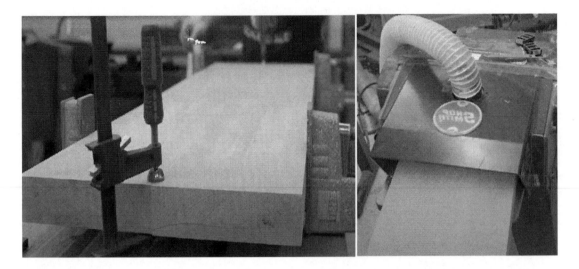

- The first joinery would be tenon on the end of the stretcher that will span between the legs.
- Use a measuring gauge to mark the tenon size and cut using a hand saw. Remove the material from the edges as marked to create a shoulder.
- After making the wedge cut, the slots are where the wedges would go inside.

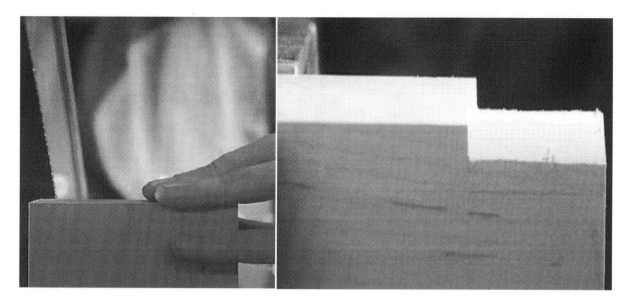

- There are many ways to make a hole. You can use driller first and chisel later to create the desired hole/mortise, as shown below. Repeat the process and make mortise and tenon on all the pieces.

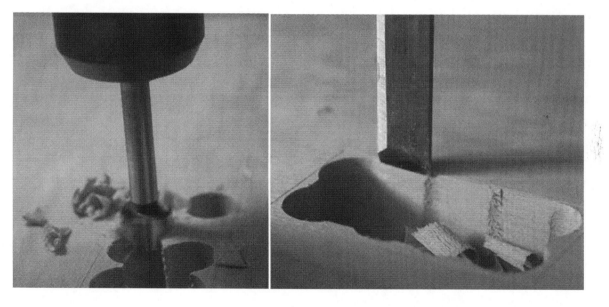

- The legs will be connected by one wood piece through a single joint and with the top lid through a double joint, as shown below.

- Make the lid as with two holes on each side and measurement as per the tenon made before.

- Put glue into all the joints after getting tenons into the mortise.
- Sand the surface.
- Apply stain/paint of your choice for finishing.

- After applying 2-3 coats of finishing, below is the final bench.

8. Glossary

Box - A corner joint with interlacing square fingers. It receives pressure from two directions.

Bridle - The bridle joint is commonly defined as the opposite of a mortise and tenon, and is also mainly used in the woodworking and even joinery professions.

The name most likely came about because it bears some similarity to the fashion in which a bit goes into an equine's mouth and is also fastened to the bridle.

Butt - Completion of a piece of timber is stuck versus one more piece of wood. This is the simplest, as well as the weakest joint. Below are the types of butt joint:
a) T-butt b) end-to-end butt c) miter butt and d) edge-to-edge butt.

Glued - The glued joint is made by planing two pieces of hardwood to ensure that when positioned together, they are in contact with each other at every point. They are then typically joined with glue. These are known as a butt joint, snag joint, the slipped joint, or slapped joint.

Halved - The halved joint is often referred to as half-lapping. It is formed after halving the two pieces, i.e., by cutting half the depth of the wood away. There are, however, exceptions to this regulation, as in the case of "three-piece halving" (or, as it is in some cases called "third lapping") and in the halving of lumber with rebated or built edges. Halving is just one of the easiest methods of linking two wood pieces, precisely where it is desired to make frames.

Lap - Completion of a piece of timber is laid over and linked to another piece of wood. Because of a large area of long-grain to long-grain timber as well as adhesive surface insurance coverage, this is a very solid joint.

Mitering - The term mitering is normally used to signify the kind of joint used at the corner of an image frame; or where two pieces of timber are beveled away so as to fit each other, as the skirting or plinth mold. In these cases, the hardwood is cut to ensure that the joint goes to 45 degrees to the face, and also, the two pieces, when put together, develop an angle of 90 levels (a right angle).

Mortise and Tenon - A mortise and a tenon joint is a kind of joint that links two pieces of wood or other material. Woodworkers all over the world have used it for hundreds of years to join timber, mainly when the adjoining wood pieces attach at an angle of 90 °. In its basic form, it is both simple and solid.

Saddle - The "saddle joint" is used for connecting upright messages to heads of the framework, and definitely takes its name from its resemblance to how the saddle fits the steed. It does not damage the framework as a mortise and tenon joint does, and shrinkage has little impact upon the joint.

Headscarf - The approach known as "scarfing" is used for the joining of lumber towards its size, making it possible for the worker to create a joint with a smooth or flush look on all its faces. One of the simplest forms of the scarfed joint is known as a half lap.

Tongued as well as Grooved - The tongued and grooved joint is used throughout the entirety of the woodworking trades, as it does, a great range of work from the laying of flooring boards to the construction of cabinets, bookcases and also various other cabinet work. As the name of the joint indicates, on one board, a groove is created, on the joining board, a tongue is produced, and the two are matched with each other.

Batten
A slim strip of timber.

Beaded timber.
A basic round molding. Likewise, see molded wood.

Bevel
An angle, however, not an ideal angle. A sloping or canted surface area.

Casing
The lumber cellular lining of a door opening.

Cellular wood panel
Comparable to blackboard and batten board panels but the battens and laths create the core and are spaced either parallel or in lattice type. Panels are relatively light yet have some strength.

Chamfered
The sides have been removed lengthwise at an angle.

Cup
To bend as a result of shrinkage, particularly across the width of a piece of timber.

Dado
The lower part of an indoor wall, usually specified with a molded rail.

Thickness
The mass of a substance, generally shown in kg/cubic meters.

Distortion
Change in wood or timber-based material caused by shrinkage as the timber dries out. This includes bowing, twisting, and cupping.

Dovetail
One-piece has a splayed shape - like a dove's tail - and fits into the second piece's socket or eye.

Doweling
Round piece or length of timber. Also known as finished wood.

Drip groove
A groove cut or molded in the underside of a door or window sill to stop rain running back to the wall.

Dry board
See Damp handling.

Edge and end spacing
Spacing's in between bolts and the sides as well as ends of the parts that are being joined.

End grain
The revealed face of hardwood created when it's punctured a plane that's vertical to the grain.

End-jointed
See Finger-jointed.

Finger-jointed
Also called end-jointed. Much shorter pieces of wood are joined to create a much longer piece. The joint resembles interlaced fingers.

Grain
The basic direction of timber fibers or the pattern generated on the surface of lumber by cutting through the fibers. Also, see End grain and Brief grain.

Groove
A long slim channel. Likewise, see Tongued as well as grooved.

Kerf
The groove cut by a saw.

Knot
The remains of a branch in wood. A branch sawn off near the trunk naturally creates noise or a live knot. A busted branch stub that comes to be surrounded by brand-new growth produces a loosened or dead knot in the hardwood.

Mitre
Two pieces of wood form an angle or joint created between two pieces of timber by cutting bevels at equal angles in the ends of each wood.

Rotating cut

The log is installed in a large lathe and turned against the blade, which peels off the veneers in long sheets. Additionally called peeling or cutting.

Tenon

The end of the wood that's been lowered in section to suit a recess or cavity of the exact same size or a forecasting tongue on the end of a piece of wood which matches an equivalent mortise.

Tongue

A decrease in the thickness of the edge of a board. Also, see Tongued and also grooved.

V- jointed

Generally, tongued and grooved wood with a V-shaped channel in the facility of the board.

Veneer

A slim or fine sheet of timber created by rotary-cutting, peeling or cutting.

Woodblock

Timber block is a floor covering made from little strips or blocks of timber, around three inches wide and nine inches long, prepared in herringbone, basket-weave, and various other geometric patterns.

Timber planks

Planks in long sizes with sizes of four inches or more.

Timber strip

Narrower and shorter boards than planks and have up to three strips of wood per board.

9. Conclusion

So this brings us to the end of our current discussion on wood joinery. We have discussed traditional joinery, Japanese joinery, and CNC joinery. No matter which form you use, the concept remains the same.

Finally a few tips for beginners:

- Avoid working with freshly cut lumber, as this will shrink after the joint is assembled. Use wood that has dried and is ready for the outside environment in which the finished product will be used.

- When making a furniture piece that will need to bear a heavy load, use bigger joints or joints with bigger architectural natures, such as twin mortise-and tenons. This will certainly distribute the load over a broader location and reduce stress on the joint. If the layout of a piece limits using big joints, utilize a number of smaller sized joints to spread out the weight as well as lower stress

- Make sure the parts of a joint are effectively proportioned. If a tenon in a mortise-and-tenon joint is too thick, the mortise participant will be weakened

- When setting up the mating boards of a joint, think about the grain direction of the elements, and oriented woods to make up for the wood activity.

- Cut the components of a joint parallel to the grain.

- For some joints, such as dovetails, utilize the completed part of the joint (the pins) to format the mating part to make it accurate.

- Make use of the proper measuring and marking devices for making joints.

- If a joint requires support, use glue along with fasteners, dowels, biscuits, or splines.

This brings the end of our discussion. I hope you liked the content. I would appreciate it if you could share your feedback and reviews on the platform. You can also reach me at valueadd2life@gmail.com.

Practice safely!

Stephen

Woodturning for Beginners Handbook

The Step-by-Step Guide with Tools, Techniques, Tips and Starter Projects

Stephen Fleming

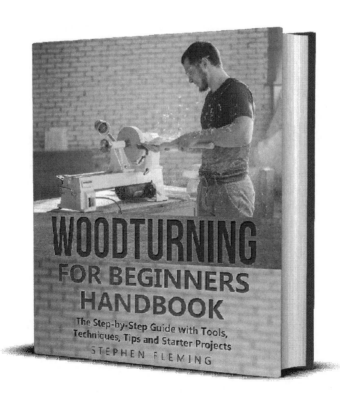

Bonus Booklet

Thanks for purchasing the book. In addition to the content, we are also providing an additional booklet consisting of Monthly planner and Project Schedule template for your first project.

It contains valuable information about woodworking and leather craft.

Download the booklet by typing the below link.

http://bit.ly/leatherbonus

Cheers!

Table of Contents

Word of caution

Woodturning can turn dangerous as I have seen and heard about many unfortunate accidents while turning; therefore, the utmost priority should be given to safety and security while practicing this activity.

I will share all my experience in this book, but it is essential to remember that, just like various other kinds of woodworking, woodturning is naturally risky.

Failure to use devices and tools appropriately or not adhering to recommended safety standards could result in significant injury or death.

It's your responsibility to make sure you understand your tools and devices and how to use them properly before attempting a woodturning task.

Make sure to read, recognize, and adhere to the most current guidelines and safety precautions for your lathe and various other devices.

Any book, video, or any other means of learning can't replace learning physically from an expert. These forms of information are only additional guidance to be used along with a practical demonstration and training from an experienced woodturner.

All the projects mentioned are my way of doing it. The same projects can be executed differently by other woodturners. So use any technique at your own risk.

So to sum it up: The first and foremost tip is to wear all the safety equipment and follow safety guidelines every time you practice woodturning.

PREFACE

"If you don't blow up a bowl now and then, you are not aren't trying hard enough"- D. Raffin, Master Woodturner

When I first started woodcraft, I looked desperately for a go-to guide about the processes and tools I would need.

The content I found online was total information overload and wasn't presented sequentially. The books I looked at were either focused on just a few processes or assumed that I already had the necessary information. A lot of the books were also very dated.

There are two ways of learning; one is learning from SMEs (Subject Matter Experts) with years of experience, and the other is to learn from people who are just a few steps ahead of you in their journey.

I fall into the latter group. I have spent five years on this hobby and am still learning from the experts.

I still remember the initial doubts I had and the tips that helped me.

This book is for those who are still running their first lap (0-3 years) in wood-crafting and want to have a holistic idea of the processes and tools they need.

I have included photographs of realistic beginner projects, and I will explain the processes and standard operating procedures associated with them.

In the last chapter, I have provided tips for beginners and a glossary of woodturning terms.

Cheers, and let's start the journey.

Stephen Fleming

1. Introduction to Woodturning

What is Woodturning

Woodturning is the art and craft of developing designed wood items on a lathe.

The lathe is a device initially created over 3,000 years ago, that holds and rotates a material like timber or rock to ensure that it can be rapidly carved with sharp tools.

Woodturned items vary from the baseball bat, chair ad table legs to rolling pins, ritualistic bowls, and also modern-day sculpture.

Woodturning is an enjoyable art - the procedure moves quickly, and shavings fly as the woodturner works. Turning is an exciting process at many levels: it is a pleasant task to learn, and with a little bit of effort, the beginner can soon end up with some excellent things.

Becoming a woodturner needs a method as well as a deep understanding of the properties of various types of timbers, the constant improvement of a technique, knowledge of surfaces, as well as a solid determination to learn the basics and make something you like.

Lathes range tremendously in dimension, from a small watch manufacturer's handheld lathe to lathes over a hundred feet long for making masts. Lathes can be powered by a motor, water, or a human, but they all execute the very same task: spinning timber so that it can be sculpted. From a single machine in the hands of the competent turner, comes a vast and remarkable selection of items.

As we know now, woodturning is shaping the wood while it rotates. The timber can be spinning at a very fast rate, so there are threats involved. It's a great idea to think about safety and security first.

Introduction to Woodturning Terminologies

1. Personal Protective Equipment (PPE)

I understand that PPE (Personal Protection Equipment) can sound boring, but it is essential. Additionally, it's not that boring, and the coolest woodturners must have the best PPE.

Eye protection: I wear a visor that offers a good deal of security from prospective accidents. A visor is likewise a fantastic option if you are like me and wear glasses.

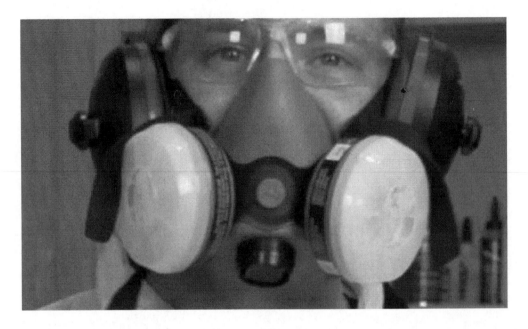

The second-best choice for keeping your eyes safe and risk-free are safety glasses. These are ideal for clarity of vision. I prefer to keep an extra pair for an emergency.

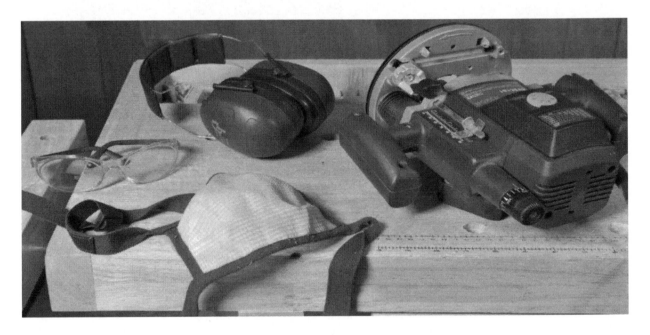

Foot protection: This isn't discussed much, but things could end up badly if you dropped something sharp on your foot.

Durable footwear will shield your feet from falling tools.

Boots or similar shoes with a steel toecap will do a much better job keeping all your toes safe.

Lung protection: This is often a somewhat overlooked aspect, but very important. Wood dust can cause asthma, which carpenters and joiners are four times more likely to get compared with other similar workers.

You can opt for a respirator with good quality filters. A proper respirator will not be uncomfortable to use and will keep your airways functioning well.

You can also get a dust extraction system. They are noisy but useful tools. The best thing about the system is that you can hook them to different shop machines, and this will remove wood dust from the area.

2. Lathe Security

I have mentioned this already, but it's essential to make sure you understand:

Woodturning can be hazardous; unlike most tools in a workshop where things cutting the timber move a little bit, the wood is rotating very quickly, so you need to think seriously about security.

We can minimize the threats, but they are still most likely to exist in some form or other, so always be careful around power devices and try to think ahead about what you are about to do and also what might go wrong.

- **Speed**

I would always advise you to start turning at a slower rate and gradually speed your lathe up until it is going fast enough to function properly. If you turn something that is not correctly balanced, it is most likely to trigger your lathe and the timber to vibrate. The more significant and more out of equilibrium, the more noticeable this issue will be, and the more likely it is that the timber will break and be flung far from the lathe. You'll be glad you are wearing a visor/screen if it hits your face. Better to damage the visor than your flesh.

If you have something huge and out of balance, you can start at a slow rate and create a balance gradually by shaving timber off one side. This will make the work a lot better balanced before you boost the speed.

3. The Tool Set

Woodturning requires a few tools, along with a lathe. I would suggest a newbie get a basic set at first, and discover just how to utilize them before adding to your collection.

 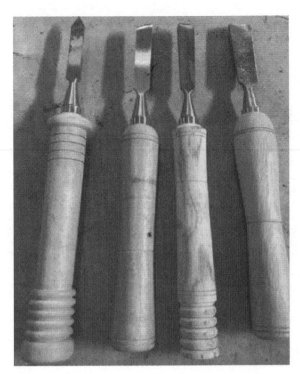

There are a great number of different turning devices out there as well as a lot of different grinds or adjustments you can do to impact the performance of your tools. Don't worry if you don't have them all to start with.

4. The Lathe

See the picture of the lathe with different parts.

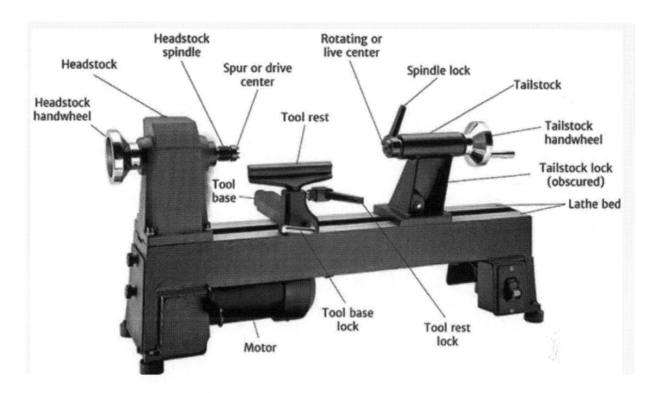

The large one: This is the one that transforms the timber. All the parts of this tool are necessary. Yet possibly the most crucial is the on-off button.

Head supply: This is the part where all the power originates.

Drive center: There are different kinds that aid in holding a job when pin turning (Pin job is transforming between centers- (the head and tailstocks).

Tailstock: The tailstock holds an online facility -comparable to a driving facility yet allows it to rotate.

Banjo and tool rest: The banjo holds the tool rest for permitting it to be transferred to the ideal position.

Turning: The device remainder allows acquisition for your turning tools to work. You rest the cutting tool on this when turning. Without the tool remainder, your devices would knock into the lathe bed and have a high probability of harming on your own or damaging your workshop.

Lathe bed: the bottom part of the lathe is the tailstock, and also banjo can slide up and down and be locked into the area as required.

237

5. Chuck

A chuck is a specialized sort of clamp made to hold an item with radial proportions, particularly a cylindrical tube. In drills as well as mills, it holds the revolving tool, whereas, in lathes, it holds the revolving workpiece. On a lathe, the chuck is installed on the spindle, which revolves within the headstock.

6. Spindle Roughing Gouge

It is a large tool transferring most of the weight.

It makes a rough shape but leaves a reasonable finish.

If you want to turn a square blank and make it round, the spindle roughing gouge is the best tool to use.

Avoid using this tool to make a bowl as there is a risk of breaking down due to its weak point going into the handle.

Spindle Roughing Gouge

- Used for roughing spindles to round
- Weak at the tang
- Not recommended for use on bowls

Roughing out

This is the best tool for roughing out the surface, so it is aptly named.

Always follow the golden rule: cut from high points to low points.

Also, use a stance where you can move easily, allowing your body to run the tool.

7. Spindle Gouge

This tool is used to make beads, curves, and can be made use to form spindle work without much hassle.

Spindle gouge

If you have used the roughing gouge, this is used similar but is a much smaller size. Beveling the spindle gouge before use still applies.

With this tool, you may wish to think about placing in some other shapes like beads as well as curves.

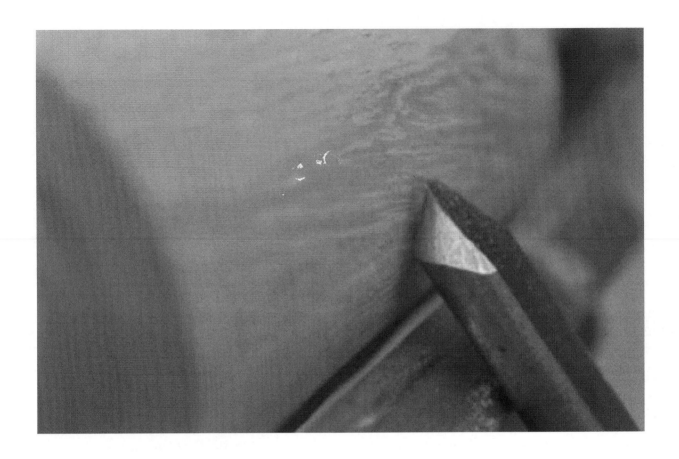

8. Skew Chisel

Mainly used as a device for planing the wood, it transforms the wood surface, making it very smooth, so it needs practically no sanding.

It can be used to develop detailing, and it can be utilized for many other tasks.

This device has a reputation for being tough and challenging to handle. But as soon as you understand how to use it properly, it will be a beneficial tool.

If you focus your complete attention on this tool, it will only take a little while to get used to it. I, too, had my share of accidents with this tool, and now I understand that the skew chisel demands total focus.

When using, it is imperative to make use of the middle part of the blade. If you strike the revolving timber with the end parts, they are likely to catch and ruin your work. This isn't the end of the world. However, it can be a little scary if you're not expecting it.

The skew chisel can be used to do a variety of things; however, it tends to be recognized for its capacity to offer planing cuts. I like to adjust my tool rest to make the wood as level as possible.

9. Parting Tool:

One of the fundamental tools in the woodturning collection is the parting tool.
 It is manufactured in lots of sizes, yet if asked by newbie, I would advise the 6mm (1/4in) identical parting tool.

The basic operation of this tool is to part or divide the timber into two separate pieces; however, it is made use of primarily to make sizing cuts, such as fillets on pin turning or spigots for chucking techniques. The parting device has lots of uses and also is an important part of any type of woodturning basic tool kit. As with any kind of device, it will only cut efficiently when it is sharp.

The parting tool is without question the simplest tool to develop as the side is short; however, the bevel is long. When sharpening the parting tool, it needs to be ground square at the end rather than at a skewed angle.

10. Bowl Gouge

As the name suggests, bowl gouge is a hand tool used to cut and form timber bowls on a lathe. The bowl gouge includes a handle linked to a sturdy steel shaft.

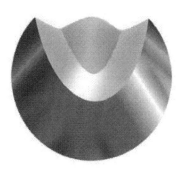 

Bowl Gouge   Spindle Gouge

11. Swept Back Grind Bowl Gouge

This is virtually like a regular bowl gouge yet the end is different

A bowl gouge has a straight work; a swept-back grind is even more of a U shape that enables the wings of the tool to be used as cutting edges.

This makes the device very flexible, enabling a better range of cuts.

This bowl gouge provides you with more options, mostly due to the wings.

While making a dish with the swept-back bowl gouge, you can utilize the wings for cutting and then dragging back to the edge of the bowl.

If you do not rub the bevel, you could risk a catch, or the tool may cut a lot more aggressively than you were initially anticipating.

12. Scraper

Scraper- these come in various profiles and act in a comparable way to a cabinet scraper.

Some turners truly love them while others do not.

The major disadvantage of using a scraper is preparing the device with a cutting burr.

I have watched timber turning video clips where the turner used only a scraper. The device is really for finessing instead of doing the heavy training.

13. Sharpening Your Tools

I think the one thing that truly pays off when turning is making sure you have sharp tools.

Sharp tools make woodworking enjoyable as it takes away the unnecessary work and gives you much better results.

There are many sharpening systems around with associated jigs to guarantee you can reproduce specific grinds.

I would recommend discovering exactly how to utilize your sharpening system for your tools- each method will be a little different.

14. Types of Turning

There are two main types of turning. Spindle Turning and Face Work.

The techniques utilized are somewhat interchangeable; however, there are distinctions to remember.

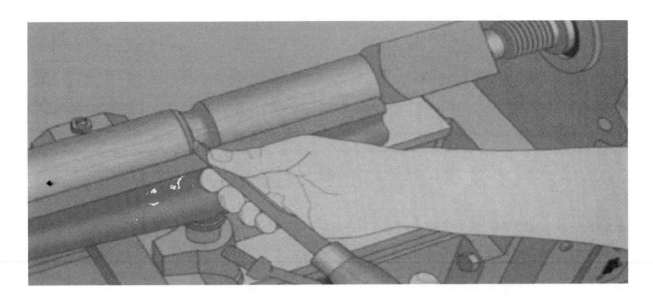

Spindle Turning

If the grain of the wood remains in line with the spindle or bed of the lathe, it is called Spindle Turning. It does not matter if you are making a chair leg or a flower holder; this is still Spindle turning.

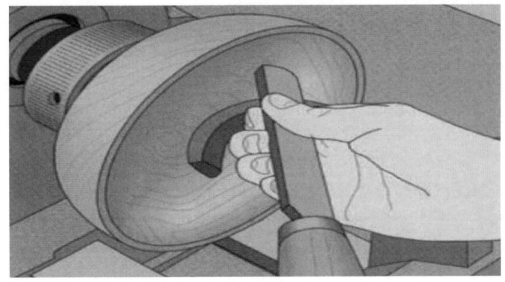

Face Work

If the grain of the timber is at right angles to the lathe axis, then this is called Face Work. A lot of bow turning is a face job.

These definitions are necessary since they establish which tools will be used for a project.

15. Sanding & Finishing

Sanding

It is much easier to do the sanding as part of the woodturning process. This step is messy, so ideally put on a dust mask and also use a dust extractor.

The dos

Develop the grit. The lower the number on an item of sandpaper, the more aggressive it is. Depending on your skills with the tools, you may intend to use coarse paper to hide mistakes, yet even if you don't, you might have some changes that could need a little easing.

The grit dimension of sandpaper is the number, which is inversely related to the fragment dimension. A small number such as 20 or 40 indicates a coarse grit, while 1500 shows a fine grit.

Modification Directions: You could be tempted to allow the lathe to do all the jobs; however, this might not offer the most effective results. The grit of the sandpaper may make red stripes; to stop this from happening, stop the lathe after you finish each grit. This will separate all the unwanted lines.

Finishing

The important thing is to think about how your object is going to be utilized. If it's likely to be used and washed a whole lot, you might want to think about a melamine/ plastic or even CA surface finish.

If it will be used with food or is a plaything, you will need to find a safe or food-safe coating. If you desire a finish that is easy to apply, you could use an oil coating like Danish oil or perhaps wax.

You might additionally want to think about coloring the project.

About Wood: Wood Toxicity and Ways to Protect Yourself

Generally, there are three groups of wood toxicity: irritability, sensitization, and poisoning.

Inflammation/Irritation

Skin, breathing tracts, and mucous membranes are often aggravated by any fine dirt or sawdust because it takes in moisture, consequently drying out the surface area with which the dirt is in contact.

Itchy skin, and sneezing, are two examples of fundamental inflammation of fine sawdust. The degree of irritation is equal to the exposure time and the concentration of wood dust.

However, irritability is not always benign. Woods like walnut and rosewood emit pleasant odors with low levels of dirt, which most woodworkers associate with being just one of the advantages of dealing with timbers. Nevertheless, the natural compounds in these woods that cause the aromas are also possibly toxic with higher dosage and direct exposure.

The long-term results of exposure to wood dust can include allergies to the dust or, potentially, nasal cancer.

Sensitization

Materials in timber that trigger a rising allergy after frequent exposure is called sensitizers.

This kind of toxicity is specific to people and takes time to establish - some individuals may experience a considerable reaction to the wood while others do not.

While sensitization generally requires time and repeated direct exposure to create, it is feasible for some people to have an allergic reaction to a timber upon their first exposure to it.

Even if you do not respond to a timber (or its dust) the first couple of times you are exposed to it, it's still vital that you take precautions and stay clear of as much direct exposure as possible. Your body is more likely to establish a reaction the more you are exposed.

Poisoning

250

Widely dangerous chemicals are hardly ever discovered in all-natural timber that's available on the business market.

Most poisons in plants and trees are located in the bark and/or sap-- there are some exceptions for rare woods.

In some cases, harmful chemicals are present in timber items, such as when the wood is pressure-treated wood for kitchen cabinetry, flooring, or furniture.

Some more common timber demands that woodworkers understand their own allergies. Those that have an allergic reaction to aspirin must avoid using timbers from birch and willow trees (Betula spp. and Salix spp.) because these have a good amount of salicylic acid, the essential active ingredient in aspirin.

Prevention

You can limit your exposure to wood dust by complying with the following points.

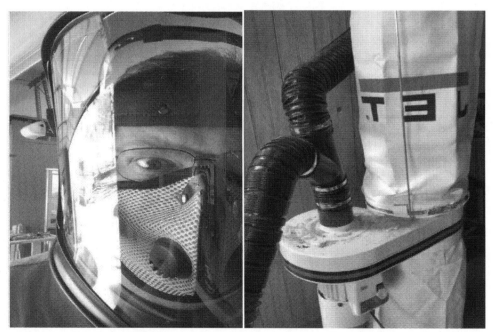

Safety Gear   Dust Collector

1. Usage a vacuum cleaner for dirt collection in your workshop, as well as making sure your shed is aerated with fresh air.

Dust Collector

2. Use safety devices while woodworking: dust mask, goggles or a full-face respirator, and also a protective barrier such as lotion. Apply lotion to arms or exposed skin.

3. As soon as you have finished woodworking, change your garments, wash them, and take a shower. This will certainly prevent wood dust from being transferred to your home, where you or your household would be repeatedly subjected to it.

What about the toxicity of wood in my finished project?

"Not to omit any one of them, the yew is similar to these other trees in general appearance. It is an ascertained fact that travelers' vessels, made in Gaul of this wood, to hold wine, have caused the death of those who used them."

–Pliny the Elder, from *Naturalis Historia*, ca. 77 AD

Infant baby cribs and also food utensils are frequently projected that woodworkers are interested in, and that needs to be made from 'safe' woods and finishes. In short: a sealed and finished wood poses no risk of poison.

What sealant or finish should you use? Solvent-based finishing items (lacquer, varnish, etc.) are highly hazardous in their fluid state, yet when used and dried, both finishes are completely safe.

For projects such as salad bowls and cutting boards that will be in contact with food, you truly don't desire a hard shell finish (lacquer or varnish) that can chip or rub off. Mineral oil, teak oil, and butcher block oil are all common and secure selections for these projects.

**Link to the full list of wood allergies and toxicity https://www.wood-database.com/wood-articles/wood-allergies-and-toxicity

WOOD SPECIES	REACTION	AREA(S) AFFECTED	POTENCY
Abura	irritant, nausea, giddiness, and vomiting	👁	★★☆☆
African Blackwood	irritant, sensitizer	✋👁👃	★★★☆
Afrormosia	irritant, nervous system effects, asthma, splinters go septic	✋👁👃	★★★☆
Afzelia	irritant, sneezing	✋👁👃	★★☆☆
Agba (Gossweilerodendron balsamiferum)	irritant	✋	????
Aglaia (Aglaia genus)	irritant	✋👃	★★☆☆
Ailanthus	irritant	✋	★☆☆☆
Albizia	irritant, nausea, pink eye, giddiness, nose bleeds	✋👁👃	★★★☆
Alder (Alnus genus)	irritant	✋👁👃	★☆☆☆
Alligator Juniper	irritant	✋👃	★★★☆
Amboyna	irritant, asthma	✋👃	????
Andiroba	irritant, sneezing	✋👁👃	★★☆☆

Reference: wood-database.com

253

2. Process & Techniques

Wood Turning Types

Green Turning: Turning freshly cut timber that has a high moisture content is called Green Turning.

It is simple, as devices quickly cut the timber and create less dust.

Nonetheless, since wood contracts as it dries out, a green turning may warp or fracture.

Some turners deliberately allow the timber to misshape so that each completed piece has a unique form. Others try to lessen the distortions by turning a piece twice.

The first turning is done when green, leaving optimum thickness so that it dries out well. The second round happens after it is dry, and gives the final shape.

All-natural edge turning: An item that includes the outer tree trunk or limb as its side.

Imaginative turnings and natural-edge things made using this technique are typically bowls or hollow vessels.

Multiaxis Turning: The method of turning a solitary piece numerous times, utilizing various sets of centers each time. You can remount the job item by hand or utilize a unique chuck that can be used to hold the workpiece off its exact center.

Ornamental Turning: This is an approach that calls for a specialized machine called a rose engine lathe. The piece is placed on a rocking headstock, and a spinning tool cuts unique and ornamental patterns.

Segmented Turning: Any turning that includes numerous tiny items of wood in its layout. Segmented turnings consist of ones where the entire turning is made from sections and those where just a small portion of the turning is fractional. Larger segmented turnings can consist of several thousand pieces of wood, all precisely cut and assembled to form unique layouts or pictures.

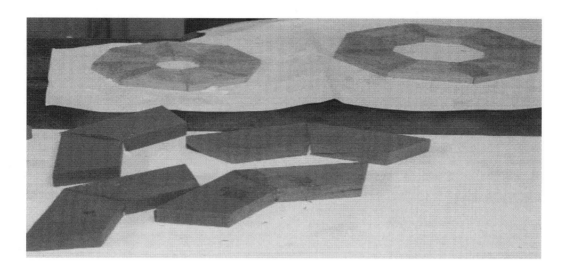

What do you require to start woodturning?

You require something that will rotate timber. A tiny beginner's lathe is an excellent option; you don't need a huge, strong lathe to start with. One more choice is to make your very own lathe using a drill or a drill press if you're feeling creative.

What's the distinction between a huge and a small lathe?

Mini Lathe   Large Lathe

Generally, the size of the wood to be turned decides which type of lathe to use.

If you wish to turn bigger pieces, then a larger lathe is needed. For example, smaller sized desk lathes can turn about 10 inches in size, whereas bigger lathes can turn up to 24-inch bowls.

The bed length is an additional distinction. Bigger lathes have longer bed lengths; however, many smaller lathes also come with an extension.

A bigger lathe will certainly be sturdier and can also deal with extra-large items of wood without shaking. Nonetheless, if you secure your lathe appropriately and use moderately sized items of wood, you won't have much of a concern, regardless of what size lathe you have.

What accessories do you require?

Most lathes come with a faceplate, a spur center, and a live center for the end, and that's all you need to get started other than the turning tools.

Do you require a chuck?

Chuck

Well, it depends. Many individuals turn with chucks, but a lot of individuals become proficient woodturners without one. Certain items are less complicated to turn using a chuck, such as hollowed-out boxes and bowls; however, there are many other items you can turn that you don't need a chuck for.

What kind of devices do you require?

So you have the ideal tools and modern-day carbide cutting tools. The primary difference between both is the learning curve. Carbide cutting devices are simpler to utilize at once, whereas with typical tools, it takes a bit longer to learn the right method.

Additionally, you need to hone the conventional devices with a grinder as you use them, to keep them sharp; nevertheless, that's not a problem with the carbide cutting ones, as you can change the tips when they become dull.

The two types are utilized differently. A conventional tool like a roughing gouge, for example, is held at an angle, pointing up in the direction of the timber as you're cutting, whereas the carbide devices are held directly.

What are the actions of establishing the lathe?

When you have unboxed your lathe, first of all, place in your spur center and your real-time center, and make sure they are satisfactorily in the middle on center; that is important if you do spindle turning.

One more beneficial thing is putting down some WD40 or various other lube on the bed to make everything slide more smoothly. Make sure you re-apply the lubricant every time you turn.

If you have a desk lathe, it must be screwed down to secure it.

Likewise, be sure to examine your belts, so they're on the appropriate rate of what you're attempting to do.

When do you use various speeds?

When initially establishing an item of timber on the lathe, begin slowly.

If the lathe starts to wobble, decrease the speed. Then as soon as your piece is centered, you can increase the speed.

Be aware that if you're working with an item of timber with issues in it, you intend to be much more cautious and begin the rate out slower; otherwise, it can break down.

Can you turn any kind of wood?

Fundamentally, you can turn with any timber; however, it's a great idea to steer clear of anything treated and compressed. Additionally, certain tropical woods like cocobolo and rosewood can cause some irritation. It doesn't trouble all individuals, yet some people have a worse reaction to those than others.

Also, no matter what kind of timber you're turning, it can trigger issues if you inhale the dust. Remember to wear a mask or a respirator.

Turning different timbers

While you can turn any timber, certain woods are softer to turn, and others are harder. As an example, mounting lumber is soft, whereas hardwoods like walnut and maple are harder. After that, specific timbers like applewood or cherry are also more challenging to turn than walnut but are also more beautiful when turned.

When do you turn damp vs. completely dry wood?

You utilize dry timber when you don't intend to have movement anymore after it's turned. If you're making boxes, you might use completely dry timber; by doing this, your lid does not go out of shape.

Greenwood (or wet timber) is frequently used for bowls. Initially, you rough turn when the timber is wet, then allow the dish to dry completely for about a year, and after that turn it finely once again.

Damp timber is also very different to turn than dry wood. It's much softer as well as much more comfortable to turn and a great deal more enjoyable!

Why get a lathe?

Well, woodturning opens up many doors as well as enabling you to do things that are hard to accomplish by other means. It's a great way to digitally detox and an exciting way to pass the time.

As an example, if you're making a table, you can turn round legs with various designs on them for it. Bowls and plates can be made on the lathe, in addition to spindles, baseball bats, knobs, and various other things that belong in the "round family" of items.

How to Pick a Timber for Turning

There are four major factors you can use to narrow the field when choosing timber for turning:
1. Rate/Price
2. Shade/Color
3. Durability
4. Workability

Rate/Price

This might seem obvious, yet it is a reasonable place to start.

Regardless of your woodworking understanding, you will know how much you can invest in the job; this can remove a lot of expensive alternatives that you don't need to consider.

Now, you might be thinking, " However, I have no idea what price various timbers are?".

That's fine, while I promote buying from your local timber stores when possible, you can make use of online stores as a pricing source even if you don't buy from them (and in some cases, you need to buy online since your local vendor may not have what you require).

Most likely a site like WoodWorkersSource.com or. BellForestProducts.com will have many choices, and you can also look for what size blank you need within a given price range.

This will certainly offer you a concept of what timbers you should be looking into.

When you have a checklist of hardwoods in your rate range, you can begin to choose further.

Shade/color

I'll proceed and address before you ask: yes, you can stain an item of light timber. However, this will certainly not provide you with the same look as the original colored wood, and if your piece ever gets damaged, it will show up light, but it can be a means to obtain a beautiful looking item at a lower price to start with.

Regarding shade, it will undoubtedly be only approximately what you desire for your task.

This is merely an additional qualifier than can help thin out a substantial sea of great options.

If you wish to make an item of wood darker, several choices can be more suitable than staining. I'll offer you three examples:

1. Ammonia fuming: a procedure whereby wood is exposed in a contained setting to the fumes that ammonia emits as it vaporizes over a fairly brief time period. The timber will come to be considerably darker or even virtually black.

2. Burning: A darkening process where a torch scorches timber, then the black ash on the outside is swept aside, revealing a dramatically darker piece of wood below.

3. Ebonizing: This process makes use of house ingredients. The solution is made from vinegar, which has had steel wool soaking in it for several weeks. When applied to an item, it reacts to the timber's tannins to create a dark shade.

I am not a professional on these darkening approaches, and I would certainly assume they each work better on particular woods than others.

Each approach also has its associated risks, so be sure to do your research study right into each technique to guarantee you know precisely how to do it safely and even properly before attempting.

Durability

Some of the qualities of durable wood are hardness/density, rot resistance and insect resistance.

One point to note is that timber's firmness doesn't have anything to do with the category of " wood."

That classification comes from the seeds of the tree, so do not think that all wood is hard or heavy.

One of the softest timbers is balsa wood, which is classified as a hardwood.

Since we have that cleared up, it allows us to have a look at the characteristics.

Hardness/Density

To provide you with a standard, here are some common timbers you could hear of being utilized often:
Pecan:
Solidity - 1820 lb-ft.
Thickness - 46 lb/ft.

Maple:
Solidity - 1450 lb-ft.
Thickness - 44 lb/ft.

White Oak:
Solidity - 1350 lb-ft.
Density - 47 lb/ft.

White Ash:
Solidity - 1320 lb-ft.
Thickness - 42 lb/ft.

Making use of a denser timber will provide more weight to your piece, which can give it a feel of higher quality.

Making use of a harder timber will give your piece a little additional resistance to damages and also dings, which might be helpful if the part is useful as opposed to decorative.

Rot Resistance/Insect Resistance

Some timber does better with wetness and is also more insect resistant than others, hence making them preferable for outdoor and aquatic applications.

While a lot of protection can be gotten with different finishing techniques, having a wood that is a lot more naturally suited to these scenarios is never a poor thing.

Regarding these two standards, you will simply need to do a little study for every timber you are considering. This can be a great aid in choosing the right wood for a specific project to guarantee it will last a long time.

Workability

The tough or hardwood is more difficult to turn.

Here are the results of the few turnings as per our experience:

The softwoods were simpler to turn and did not blunt the devices as swiftly.

Nevertheless, even a little slip of the tool would certainly put a deep gouge in the timber.

Also, the final projects mar much more easily due to their softness.

Last but not least, you cannot turn these timbers to as tiny size as the hardwoods since they are weaker.

Few more tips

1. Raid scrap bins and also estate sales to gather a range of timbers to try and also see what you like to work with, and what you think looks good.

2. Get a notebook, and each time you turn something, list
   - What kind of timber it was and what you thought about it
   - How it turned.
   - Any type of problems like damaging or tear-out.
   - What kind of finish you used
   - Did you like it on this certain wood?

3. You can also maintain a spreadsheet containing timber species with specifications to ensure that whenever you have a task in mind, you can go to that spreadsheet, see what data is available, filter by specific standards, and hopefully select an excellent timber for the job.

3. Finishing

Sanding Tips

A well-sanded surface is a pre-requisite for high-quality finishing. Below are a few tips for sanding:

- Use high-quality sandpaper, and throw it away when it becomes dull.

- Supply raked/side lighting on the sanding surface area to get any issues.

- Sand your task through all the grits up to 320 or 400 grit without missing any.

- When you believe you are done with sanding, sand one more time with the grain (and the lathe off) to get rid of scratches across the grain.

- Please make sure you don't create heat when sanding, or you'll burnish the surface, making it hard for a finish to adhere to or penetrate.

- Clean the surface with a paper towel before applying the finish.

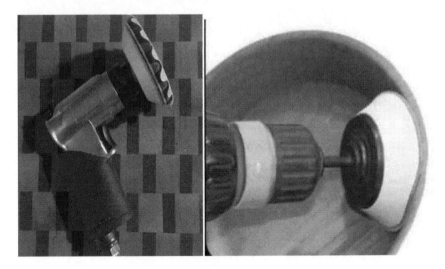

Power Sander

Finishing Options

There is no single finish suitable for all of your woodturning tasks.

So, where do you start when choosing the appropriate finishing for your project?

The criteria for choosing the ideal finishing for your turning project depends on many factors like:

- Kind of wood
- The project's size and planned use
- Sturdiness
- Drying time
- Required shine (satin or gloss)
- Ease of application
- Solvent or water-based
- Cleanup
- Repairability

Commonly, the novice will find it challenging to achieve a satisfying finish and will certainly use one finish that does it all. However, this is limiting and does not consider how wood needs to consider depending on its final usage. Is the piece purely ornamental? For food call? Or will it need a lot of managing? Are you not sure what you intend to do with the item, or do you want to reveal the beauty of the wood grain?

When viewing a turning project, it is usually the kind of finish or requirement of finish that allows the piece down.

The most significant mistake made by many is to apply too much finish and wind up with streaked or irregular finishes and improperly performed sanding. Here we aim to address these blunders.

Finishing products

Sealants

This team consists of cellulose, acrylic, and shellac ranges. The group also includes pre-catalyzed melamine lacquer, which is a waterproof sealant. These are utilized to seal the timber before using a finish, but they can be used as a final finish. Sanding sealants are diluted by 50%, making use of a suitable thinning agent to enable application over larger areas while remaining wet across the entire item. It also allows the product to flood across the whole project if needed. If left pure, it is commonly challenging to obtain an even coverage with the product directly from the tin.

Waxes

These come in various kinds, such as soft paste waxes or hard stick varieties, and those that can be colored. These are typically best used over a sealant, yet some brand-new types can be used on bare timber.

Resilient hard-wearing finishes

Lacquers and oils fit into this section thoroughly. Some can permeate the lumber; others develop a surface finish and can be found in gloss, satin or matt sheen. Oil is believed to be one of the most durable finishes, but it is not necessarily the best bet for resisting finger marks and dirt contamination.

Beeswax

Decorative finishes

The kind of finish that will customize or alter the appearance of the timber. In some cases, it may cover the product to where it no longer appears like timber. This complex group includes colored stains and also waxes that are related to bare wood along with chemicals such as bleach.

Food safe

If the piece will have contact with food, then the finish has to be food-safe, which suggests it has to comply with existing federal government requirements (if these apply). Conversely, you might utilize pure beeswax, vegetable/mineral oil or liquid paraffin, all of which are applicable, plus lots of other types of finishes your supplier can provide.

Abrasives

These ought to be treated as an additional cutting tool, and you really do get what you pay for where these are concerned. Top-quality abrasives are not low-cost; they need to be fabric-backed and flexible and must not crack when folded. These are generally made of aluminum oxide and are warmth resistant as well as waterproof to some degree. The qualities I use are 80, 120, 180, 240,

269

320, 400 grit. I usually begin sanding at 80 grit since my turning tools are sharpened on a dry grinder that is fitted with an 80 grit white aloxite grinding wheel, which generates 80 scratches per inch along the cutting edge. 80 grit abrasive will rapidly remove any type of swellings or bumps from the work surface. When working as an apprentice stonemason brightening granite, I remember that if I missed one grade, I had to begin again - there are no short cuts to an excellent finish.

Polishing cloths/papers

Some say clothes, some claim papers, yet I utilize both depending upon the task in hand. Mutton cloth is used for sanding sealer as well as polishing waxes, whereas paper is used for rubbing polish and oils. However, keep in mind that all paper towels have a rough top quality of their own, so it may take time to discover the right one for you. Beginning with a high-quality kitchen paper towel, but ensure you NEVER twist any kind of sprucing up cloth or paper around your fingers. Also, never allow loose ends to track around turning equipment or job.

Wire wool and also Nyweb/Webrax

0000 wire wool is used to reduce finishes as well as sealants. Nyweb and Webrax are synthetic forms of wire wool that do not deteriorate as quickly as the usual wire wool, and they do not leave debris behind as they are made use of. The basic method for finishing is to sand, seal, and then use the finishing coat. Nevertheless, when you are using oil, there is some change in this technique.

Sanding the outside

1. Reduce the lathe speed by half and make use of a piece of abrasive folded in two to sand the outside of your bowl. Keep in mind to maintain the rough moving, never allow it to stop in one area, or scrap it in your last finish coat. Finish the job gradually with the grit from 80-400.

2. With the lathe stationary, use a 25mm (1in) paintbrush and a generous layer of sanding sealer to the dish exterior, moving swiftly to cover the entire surface while it is all damp. Do this quickly, or one-part will dry before an additional coat causing a patchy finish.

3. With the lathe still switched off, get rid of the excess with mutton fabric. When it is dry, turn on the lathe and burnish with the cloth.

4. Making use of Nyweb to cut down the surface area to get rid of the increased grain and excess product. Repeat the process over several layers.

5. Add a moderate layer of paste wax and also allow it to dry completely. Be patient as drying times vary throughout the year.

6. Switch on the lathe and with a clean towel burnish and polish the surface area of the bowl. Move to a clean spot on the cloth first.

Finally, sand the inside

1. Use the same technique to sand the interior of your bowls, but this time around, sand the bowl in the bottom left quarter between the 6 and 9 o'clock placements.

2. Additionally, power sand the interior. Notice the angle at which the head is presented to allow just the lower edge to touch the rotating bowl

3. Attempt a larger sanding pad than you would typically make use of; the larger the pad, the more surface area contact you have - which is better suited to the distance. This larger surface area contact has the advantage of having the ability to level any surface undulations better than a smaller pad.

4. You might additionally utilize an inertia/ passive shear sander to get rid of any radial sanding marks that may still show up externally.

Approach for applying a fueled oil finishing coat

Applying oil takes time; however, it does offer the timber a much deeper sheen as well as richness. When sanding with oil, the amount of fine dust generated in the workshop is much less; it will also fill grain, leaving the wood with a much softer and warmer feel. This is optimal when making things that come into contact with food. Sand as you would typically, making sure no damage is left on the outside of the dish. When completed with oil, it is a great suggestion to cover the lathe bed. Here, I decided to use Danish oil.

1. Place a liberal layer of oil on your bowl, using a 25mm (1in) paintbrush, and leave to sit and trickle for 10 mins. During this time, the oil will soak into the surface of the wood.

2. Replenish the oil and turn on the lathe to its slowest setting. Using old 400 grit abrasive, proceed to abrade the bowl as the fining sand progresses. If it seems too thick and is not spreading properly, add a little bit more oil and continue.

3. Continue to sand the dish until there is a slurry appearing externally on the wood.

4. Wipe clean and completely dry, then run the lathe and burnish with paper. Now set the item to one side in a dust-free area and permit to dry for 24 hours. The next day includes one more layer of oil by brushing on and leaving it to sit for a while, then clean completely dry. Continue until you get the desired finish (I find that two or three coats usually are enough). Once the oil is completely dry, the bowl may well require an extra polish with a reducing substance such as wax. This often suffices to bring the piece to a perfect shine.

Friction polish

This product is usually misused by novices and must only be used on small products, such as light/cord draws and container stoppers. Most manufacturers specify that no sealant is required; however, I find this is not the case - you can achieve a much superior finishing coat when a sealant is used.

1. Sand the item as usual. Fining sand on top allows you to see what you are doing

2. Utilize a small brush to use your chosen fining sand sealer and place a little piece of mutton fabric to the rear of the item with the lathe running - this will certainly catch the excess and burnish it all at once.

3. Continue to burnish. If you have too much product on the item, much of it will be removed during this procedure.

4. Using Nyweb to cut down the surface and remove any further deposit.

5. With your brush dipped into your friction polish, apply as you did the sealant. However, this time utilize a paper towel folded in half.

6. Give the item a final polish using a clean part of the paper.

4. Safety and Best Practices

Safety Instructions

The best advice/quote on woodturning safety I came across is, ***"Over-Confidence Is a Woodturners Worst Nightmare."*** I couldn't agree more and emphasize the importance of remaining careful at all times while working. Below are the instructions:

Sample accident account 1:

"This is why you use face security. A 25 lb piece of almond just blew up and came off my lathe. My Air Tend Pro is in numerous pieces. I took the hit, yet came out with a couple of small cuts as well as a huge bump on the head. Have to admit I am frightened. The Air Trend is broken, but without it, I would have been. I will certainly boost my safety measures before resuming".

General Instructions

- Please read, understand, and follow all guidelines and safety warnings that include operating your lathe and various other devices before attempting to use them. Failing to comply with safety precautions in your devices' owner's handbooks can lead to severe injury.

- Maintain your lathe as touted in the owner's handbook. Look for damage, bad alignment, binding, and anything that might lead to trouble when you turn the lathe on.

- Do not try to run a lathe without proper training or developing a proper understanding of how it works safely.

- Never operate a lathe or any other power device if you are ill, tired, distracted, or drunk.

- Avoid unanticipated distractions. Keep children and pets away from the lathe area while you're working. Also, see to it that anyone entering the area understands not to distract your focus while the lathe is running.

- Exposure to wood dust can lead to sensitization of the skin and respiratory system, potentially resulting in severe allergic reactions after repeated or direct exposure to lower concentrations of the dust.

- Always operate in a location with appropriate airflow and wear a dust mask, respirator, or air-circulating helmet to prevent hazardous breathing dust. A respirator is an especially excellent concept when sanding and also when working with exotic timbers.

- Keep the flooring in your workspace tidy and uncluttered to prevent slipping or stumbling when you turn.

- See to it, there is sufficient light and also room to move freely.

- Wear a quality compliant face guard while woodturning. Regular spectacles do not provide appropriate security.

- Wear an appropriate hearing defense, specifically while turning.

- Please do not wear anything that might get caught in the lathe while it is running. That means no rings, watches, or other jewelry.

- Wear tops with short sleeves, or roll up long sleeves. Do not put on loose garments. Tie long hair back. Do not wear gloves while turning.

Using Turning Tools Safely

Use the tools just as they are made after reading the user manual and guidelines. Unexpected use might lead to severe injury or death. For example, you cannot use a Spindle Roughing Gouge on a bowl. Spindle roughing gouges are not built to manage the stress associated with face turning and could break, possibly causing significant injury.

Working on Lathe

- Position yourself on the appropriate side of the lathe; the timber should rotate towards you.

- Inspect the lathe speed setup before starting the lathe.

- Begin the slowly and keep it there up until the workpiece is transformed, round and balanced.

- Maintain a slow-moving rate for larger-diameter turnings. Suit the speed to the transforming project.

276

- Always shut off the lathe and allow it to come to a complete stop before changing the placement of the tool rest or tool rest holder (banjo). Never change the tool rest while the lathe is running. Never stop a rotating work surface with your hand.

- Before starting the lathe, see to it that the workpiece is mounted safely between the drive center of the headstock and the tailstock or held firmly with a four-jaw chuck. When the workpiece is protected in a chuck, use the tailstock whenever feasible as an added step of safety.

- Set the tool rest as close to the workpiece as you can, but make sure that it won't get caught in any part of the workpiece during turning. Rearrange the tool rest after removing excess timber from your project work surface to maintain needed support for your tools.

- Before starting the lathe, always rotate the workpiece by hand to see if it clears the bed of the lathe, the tool rest, and the tool rest owner (also called the banjo). Always check to see that all nuts and bolts are locked tight.

- Make sure that all guards, belt covers, and various other security attributes are correctly installed and are secure before starting the lathe. Eliminate any loosened products, tools, or unnecessary workpieces from the workspace before starting the lathe.

- Check your work surface for any divides, splits, inclusions, or various other issues that can compromise the stability of the wood and perhaps cause the work surface to come apart or come off the lathe. Do not try to turn pieces that have substantial problems.

- Continue to inspect the work surface as you turn, stopping the lathe regularly to examine for problems exposed by the elimination of the product.

- Never leave the lathe running on its own.

- Keep the turning tools sharp, which will leave a better surface and need much less pressure to cut the wood, reducing the likelihood of an injury. Never force a dull tool.

- Preserve a balanced position. Do not overreach or utilize extreme pressure to do any machine operation.

- Always keep fingers behind the tool rest when turning. Severe injury can result if your fingers get captured in between the tool rest and the turning stock.

- Use both hands to keep complete control of your turning devices, with one hand forward to regulate the cutting side and the other back.

- To decrease the likelihood of hazardous catches, always bring the tool to the device rest initially, see to it you've got it secured there, and use it to change the spinning work surface.

- Always relocate the banjo out of the way and get rid of the tool rest before fine sanding a workpiece on the lathe. If you do not, you risk obstructing your fingers or twisting your wrist.

- Never utilize a cloth to apply surface or polish while a job is rotating on the lathe. The cloth might be captured and pull your hand right into the turning, possibly causing severe injury.

Sample accident account 2 :

I was just reminded again of the relevance of wearing safety tools. The bowl I was turning came apart at one of the development rings. There were no signs when I inspected earlier.

Wood Turning Best Practices

Workspace setting

The location, particularly around your wood lathe, should be clear and without debris, devices, or any barriers. Power cords present a risk when they are straight underfoot. I keep my power cords behind the lathe, where I will not get tangled in them.

Wood shavings begin to build up and can become a threat. My woodturning coach has an ideology that a thin layer of shavings on the ground is a good thing. I have also dropped many small items like screws and hex wrenches to have them roll away completely. I have used a handheld magnetic strip on a deal to run over the shavings and relocate much of those dropped objects.

Likewise, I have a comfortable, supported anti-fatigue floor covering on the flooring where I stand while turning bowls, making my lathe turning time very comfortable. At a minimum, the anti-fatigue mat prevents my legs from feeling sore after a full day of turning. And the mat is very easy to lift as I whisk dust away from my workplace.

Wearing Safety Gear

Whenever around a lathe, it's a great habit to use safety gear. The essential woodturning safety devices are safety glasses, full face shields, safety shoes, respirators, and an efficient air filtering system.

Sample Workspace

Safety Gear

Lighting

Make sure to have a lot of good light at the lathe. A flexible light or 2 is essential to light up the straight work area. An excellent movable light, angled from the side, helps to clear up high and low places on a dish surface area. Use a flexible light such as this to brighten your lathe completely.

Woodturners physical and mental state

The state of your physical and mental being is as crucial or even more vital than whatever mechanical work you are doing.

If you aren't feeling good, are tired out or intoxicated, it's best to turn off the lathe until the next day.

Give yourself a break and don't push if your physical state might impair your judgment and motor abilities.

It can be challenging to self detect problems, as we are generally the last to admit we ought to stop. Small errors such as catches that don't usually happen can be an early sign that it is time for a break.

A woodworker working on a lathe

Working on a Lathe: best practices

Before we can begin to turn, we need to make sure the location around the lathe is well-defined and prepared.

Any added tools and products need to be well away from the maker.

Several lathes have a tool tray for chuck keys, hex wrenches, as well as other accessories underneath the bed. This is fine to utilize, and any un-needed tools can sit in the provided place, and they will not rapidly come loose.

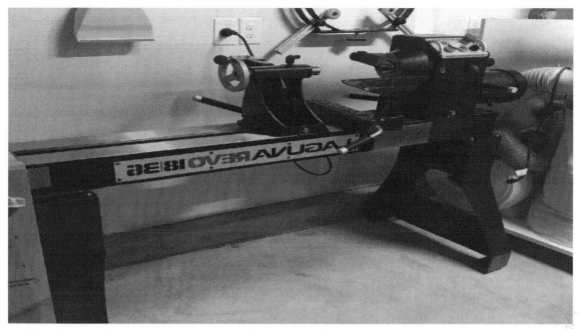

A sample lathe

Before fixing wood bowl blank to the lathe, relocate the tool rest, banjo, and tailstock, so they are entirely out of the way and make sure the power is shut off, and set the lathe speed to the most appropriate for your project.

Faceplate setting

If you choose to mount the bowl blank to a faceplate, make use of top quality timber screws and not drywall screws.

Drywall screws are much thinner and also made more cheaply compared to timber screws, and they can snap off under the high torque while transforming.

Also, make sure the screws are long enough to securely hold the bowl on place, but not so long as to hinder your desired dish shape. When your bowl space has been prepared and all set, it's time to bring it to the lathe. With the power off, rotate the dish blank by hand and watch to see if it settles away quickly.
 If this does happen, it may imply the bowl is off-center.

Faceplate mounted on wood piece

Standing clear, turn the lathe on and gradually accelerate the speed. If there is a remarkable vibration at slow-moving rates, reconsider focusing the faceplate or chuck.

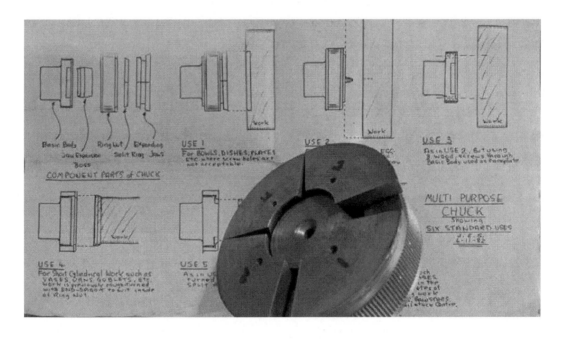

A multipurpose chuck

If the piece you're working with is off-center on purpose, understand that you will certainly have to turn the bowl at a much slower rate as a result of this inequality.

Lathe optimum speed

For checking the lathe's optimum balance speed, the general rule is to slowly boost the lathe rate until the wood piece starts to vibrate, then start decreasing the speed up until it stops shaking. That point is the optimum speed required for turning efficiently.

Check contact with a lathe.

Once the blank is placed and ready, bring the banjo and tool rest into location. With the lathe off, turn the headstock hand handles and rotate the item extensively several times to make sure no part of the dish blank will contact the tool rest, banjo, or any other part of the lathe.

Woodturner's position

Each cut made while turning a timber bowl requires to be thought out a little bit in advance. Here is an excellent method to start with when you first begin, that will progress into a habit.

I usually start by turning and forming an all-time low of the bowl from the tailstock side. While I'm doing these cuts, I do not stand in front of the lathe in the path of turning. I have had tenons stop working, sending out bowls to the flooring and bark flying off.

From the tailstock side, I usually have an excellent position to watch the action as a viewer without being in touch with any of the follies.

Even while making a leveling cut across the bottom of the turning bowl space, place most of the body to the left, or headstock side if you are right-handed, so just the arms and hands are in front of the rotating item.

Mobile Lathe

In case of a mobile lathe, move it sideways or at a place where you will find woodturning easy.

While turning to the tailstock side, bring it with you if you move to the headstock side. It requires to be in a location that can be accessed without crossing the path of the woodturning wood piece.

In case the lathe does not have this feature, and the switch is only accessible if you reach over the wood, consider stepping back from the lathe and making a broader course to the switch if something goes wrong.

Tool Rest

A tool rest is an adjustable horizontal bar for supporting a hand tool when turning.

The tool rest needs to be as close to the turning blank as the tool needs.

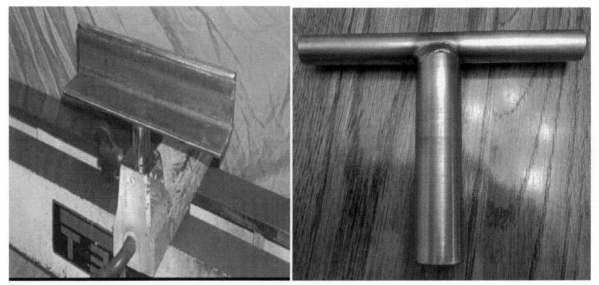

Sample Toolrest

Every tool is different, and the tool rest must be adjusted for each one.

Lathe speed

There is no perfect speed for turning a wood bowl. Yet there are some things of which to be mindful of when adjusting the speed. As a whole, I don't turn bowls any faster than 1000 r.p.m. There is hardly ever a need for speeds much quicker than this.

Sample Accident 3:

My first lathe had a rotating head so you could work straight in front of you, and I used it that way almost exclusively. This required an extension arm between the banjo and tool-rest that brought the tool-rest above the center of rotation.

I did not realize how dangerous that was. I broke two banjos, a Sorby gouge, and smashed the crap out of one of my favorite fingers more than once.

286

Stop and change the tool rest

Before moving and changing the tool rest, stop the lathe. It takes a little bit more time; however, it's far better than getting slapped by a rotating bowl on the lathe.

Keep changing the tool rest, so it is positioned to offer you the upper hand leverage, literally, as well as produce the very best cut from the tool you're using.

Finishing

When you're sanding, or whenever there are dust fragments in the air, make sure to put on a dust mask or respirator. If you are determined to turn the lathe while sanding, do so at a slow rate.

Before begin, move the tool rest, banjo, and tailstock far from the turning bowl, so they don't present a pinch point.

This is a big deal, and also I see people doing this regularly. Never use any fabric textiles to apply a finish to a **rotating bowl**. You may utilize a towel to use finishes such as oils if the lathe is off.

Instead, utilize paper towels to apply to finish products to a rotating bowl. If the paper towel gets caught, it will just rip away and create no damage.

Post Turning

Cleaning up the lathe location and put away all the tools, devices, and materials, especially the finishing materials. Dispose of used paper towels and cloths according to the manufacturer's referrals on the item packaging. Tidy up all those shavings and prepare the area for the next time it will be utilized.

4. Ten Beginner Woodturning Projects

1. Bowl

Step 1: First, a little information regarding the tools required for woodturning. Here are the devices I used on this project. There are much cheaper variations of all of these things if you are on a budget. Below is a sample of tools used for the project:

- Chuck.
- Cole Jaw Set.
- Laguna 1412, Bandsaw
- Easy Timber Devices Carbide Turning Devices.
- Lathe.

Step 2: Cut the wood

Cut your log in half lengthwise; after that, cut a square item for one of the bisections.

Mark the wood as well as place your faceplate.

Make sure to use strong screws here; drywall screws do not have a great deal of sheer toughness.

Step 3: Roughing out

To begin, rough out the bottom of your bowl.

You want to bring the outside right into shape and then start to develop the form of your bowl.

Get rid of as little material as you can, or else, you'll end up with a smaller bowl than required.

When the bottom is ready, cut a tenon and place the bowl right into your chuck jaws. Again, this may be an aftermarket product, depending on your lathe.

With the bowl on the chuck, start to rough out from within your bowl.

You want the outside as well as inside walls of your bowl to be parallel. Wall surface thickness is an individual choice.

Ensure you look for cracks in the process; logs are full of them. If you have a huge one, you can stabilize it with epoxy.

Step 4: Sand the bowl from inside

After getting the desired shape in the previous step, increase the speed of the lathe, and take shallow passes. This will result in a beautiful, smoother surface, given the tools are appropriately sharp.

Post that applies to sand to the inside surface of the bowl while it is still mounted on the lathe. You can use sandpaper from 120 to 600 grit.

 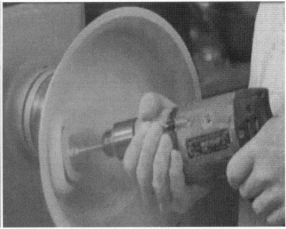

Step 5: Smooth the base of the bowl

Next off, place your bowl into a collection of Cole jaws on your chuck. There are various other methods to do this; however, Cole's jaws are quite fantastic for this kind of task.

Cutaway the tenon you created in the previous step and afterward began to make the bottom of the bowl smoother.

If the bottom is concave, the bowl will rest flat. It is essential to complete the sanding procedure once more. You could start at 80 grit in case of some more tear-out.

Step 6: Finishing

The next step is to spray polyurethane for the finish. It is simple and quick. You can also apply colors if you wish.

2. Rolling Pin

Tools Required

- Spindle gouge

- Roughing gouge

- Round nosed scarper

- Sycamore wood

- Parting Tool

- Lathe

- Take a wood plank with the dimensions as per your requirement; let's say here we take 16 inches by 3. Make sure that the tool rest is square to the bed. Ensure that everything is locked down properly before starting the lathe.

- Start with a roughing gouge. Repeat the same step at the other end to make it cylindrical.

- Now mark the handles on the cylinder on both sides. Here we take half inches from both sides and mark them as the end of the handles.

- After that, mark the handle length on both sides, as shown above.

- Use the parting tool on the half-inch marks on both sides, as shown below. (the line at the end on both sides)

- For making handles, first, use a roughing gouge and then spindle gouge, as shown in the pictures below.

- Now use a spindle gouge to make the handle of the desired same radius as the end of the handle.

- Apply sanding paper starting from 150 grit to 180 grit. Wear a respirator here and keep the paper moving all the time.

- Finish it off by applying food-safe oil rub it along the grain. Put 2-3 layers of coating.

3. Baseball Bat

Tools Required:

- 36" wood bat blank

- Wood lathe

- Turning devices

- Square

- Outside calipers

- Sandpaper

- Oil/varnish finish

- High-quality Japanese saw

Picking the wood:

Start with finding a blank of either maple or north ash. The size should be approximately 3" round and 36" long.

The straighter and tighter the grain, the much less chance it will break when you use it.

Material that's been graded for making bats is far better than what you discover at the neighborhood hardwood shop.

You can find some great sources online.

If you cannot discover a round blank, you can start with a blank that's square in cross-section.

Then chamfer the long edges to make it octagonal in cross-section.

The blank needs to be 3" longer than the final length to allow for waste at both ends.

Noting the center

The following action is to mark the center of the cylindrical tube on both sides.

You can make use of a center finder if you have one.

Otherwise, a good technique is to use a square to etch a perfect angle inside the circle.

Draw the line where the legs of the square intersect the circumference. That line will be the center.

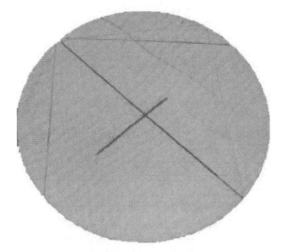

Repeat the same thing once again after revolving the square 90 degrees, as well as the intersection of those two lines is the center.

At the center, use an awl to make a hole that the centers will certainly fit into.

Roughing the blank

Mount the blank on the lathe.

I use a live facility at the tailstock and a step facility at the headstock.

I mount the bat so that the barrel will be closest to the headstock.

I locate it more comfortable to turn in this manner, and it seems to vibrate less; however, if you mount it with the barrel at the tailstock, the majority of the cuts are "downhill."

Turn the blank right into a cylindrical tube, ensuring it goes at the very least to 2.75" along with its size.

Adjust the speed to 800 rpm as it is an excellent rate.

Marking the bat

We can mark out the bat by laying pencil lines every 3" on the blank, including the end of the handle and the barrel.

Hold a pencil approximately across the spinning space as well as it will leave a clear line.

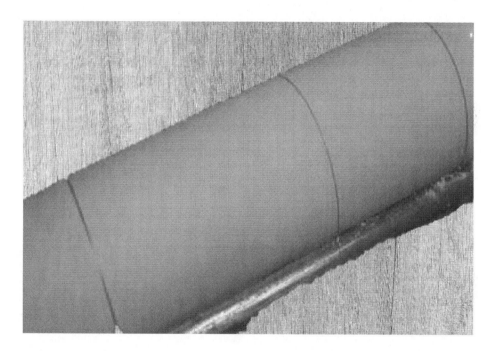

Gauging the deepness

We use a parting tool to make a small channel at the end of the barrel.

The diameter of this cut should be left at about 1/8" larger than the finished dimension.

Starting from the barrel down, cut to depth the first 3 or 4 of these marks

You can add about 1/16" to the measurement for cutting and sanding. Using a parting chisel, cut the blank until the caliper barely slips through.

Forming/shaping the barrel

The roughing gouge can be used again to eliminate a lot of the waste between the cuts.

Next, turn the lathe up to 1200-1600 rpm.

I try to keep a fair contour between the cuts by focusing on the rear of the barrel's silhouette.

I then use a skew cut to smooth the surface area.

While I'm pointing out the tools I make use of, other transforming devices can work just as well.

I usually sand the barrel with 100 grit sandpaper (or whatever the surface coating requires) before I go on to cut the remainder of the bat.

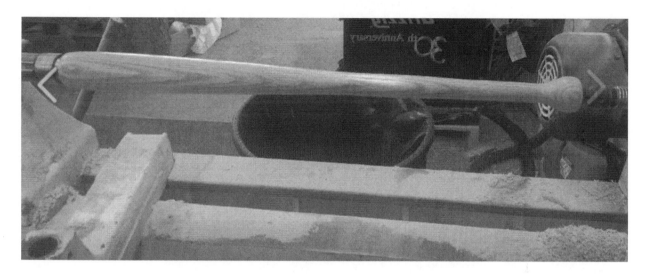

This enables me to get a great of surface area sanded before the bat becomes too whippy on the lathe.

Making the handle and knob

Continue utilizing the parting tool to note the suitable depth of the cuts.

 Utilize the spindle gouge, or the skew sculpt to level the curve in between the networks cut with the parting gouge.

The shapes and sizes of handles vary greatly and are a matter of personal choice-- they don't impact the efficiency.

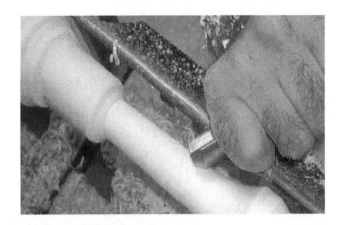

Sanding

Depending on the surface quality and level of the contour, you'll need different amounts of sanding.

If the surface area is rough and the profile not perfectly smooth, you need to begin with 80 grit sandpaper.

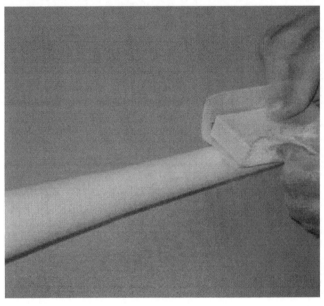

To help smooth the form and also not make the flaws even worse, it's useful to place a small block of wood inside the sandpaper, so you're not merely brightening the tops and also valleys.

If the surface area is smoother, you can start sanding with 100 or 120 grit sandpaper.

I generally sand in numerous steps up to 220 but have been cured of trying to sand it smoother by viewing how my kids throw the bats around and cover them with yearning tar.

Finishing:

A blend of oil and varnish seems to be the best finish. You can acquire these sorts of coatings in the equipment shop or make your very own combination.

You can place a couple of coats of finish on while the bat is still mounted on the lathe.

I load a dust cloth up with the combination and hold it up to the rotating bat.

Trimming the ends

Use the skew chisel held vertically to make very clean cuts on the end grain.

If you're making use of a gouge or a scarping tool, take care here because tidying up the marks left in the long run grain is most difficult.

After that, get rid of some excess with a parting chisel and also leave a shoulder for the saw to ride on.

Cut the projection on top of the barrel to about an inch across.

303

After that, remove the bat from the lathe, use small Japanese saw to cut off the little nubs, and then sand the ends.

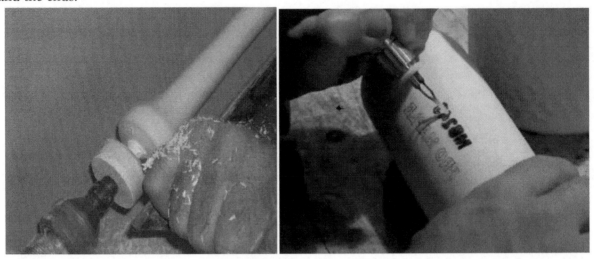

The last action is to use even more coating. I usually wet sand the surface now with 400 grit sandpaper as well as do as numerous layers as my persistence or children allow before one of them wants to take it out and hit with it.

4. Wood Canteen

Tools Required

- A robust lathe with a faceplate

- A big drill bit (around 1") and also a way to transform it

- A transforming cut carve

- A straight transforming chisel

- Sandpaper

- A saw

- Wood

- Glue

- Wood coating

Drill and Set the Center

The first step is the standard woodturning procedure.

Drill the mouth of the bottle initially and utilize it to establish the centers.

This will certainly ensure you are starting with a concentric form with the mouth in the precise center.

For example, you can use a scrap of 6" x6" Douglas fir.

The very first turning has to be finished up smoothly at this step.

Sand and do whatever else to complete this surface area, you will certainly not be remounting it again.

Removing the Shanks

The piece must then be remounted to bowl-out the interior from one side.

You can use a bandsaw to cut off items from two sides, giving a flat mounting surface for the faceplate.

Conserve those two shanks of timber; you will be making use of at least one of them to top the large opening you will now bore in the side of the container.

Bowling-out the Inside

This action is the same as bowl-turning, other than you will be turning an asymmetrical item. If your lathe has rate control, ease into it.

You can safely rough-cut a piece such as this at 700rpm.

Your chisel will wish to stray from the center, so make your cuts carefully and perpendicular to the surface you're cutting into.

Start from the boundary and move in towards the center, resisting the outward force.

If you drilled the mouth sufficiently deep, you need to break through to it.

When dealing with complicated wood, you can leave a lot of thinner walls.

If you have the skill and also a proper square carve, make an action on the edge of the dish to far better seat the cap in the future.

Make it Attractive

This next action is much more decorative than anything else, though it will include some balance to the piece, and all noticeable surface areas will have been turned.

The jug must be turned around so you can function on the opposite side. You can screw the faceplate to the containers inside the wall surface; however, only if the screws do not strike your chisel as it digs into the item.

Turning the Cap

Remember those shanks you removed in Step 2?

You will be using one, preferably the one from the side that was hollowed.

Glue it to a block of timber and install it on the faceplate.

Turn it sufficient to make it perfectly round and provide it a lip to better seat inside the jug's hollowed bowl.

Use calipers to get the right measurements.

If you have threading devices, this would be an excellent opportunity to use them, though threads might make it challenging to get the grain direction to match. Cut the cap off the block.

The sawn surface does not need to look great since it will get on the jug within the jug. It merely offers it a quick sanding.

Finishing

If you wish to make this a functional canteen, utilize a food-safe coating like pure tung oil on the inside and outside.

There are other safe finishes available, though they do not have the durability and damp resistance you would certainly want for the inside of a liquid vessel.

5. Candle Holder

Tools Required:

- Maple wood

- Waste woodblock

- Lathe

- Glue

- Roughing gouge

- Wax and Mineral Oil

- Sandpaper

Steps

- Glue the piece of maple on the waste block, as shown below. Leave it for few minutes and then start the turning process.

- Measure the radius of the candle on the back of the maple wood piece to make a fitting hole on it.

- Now give a slant shape to the wood piece using scraper and gouge as shown below till the shape becomes like the picture shown below.

- The next step is sanding and then put on finishing wax and mineral oil.

- Remove the wood piece and see the candle slot. Then put it back on the lathe to work on the bottom side of the candle holder. Apply sanding and finishing to this surface also done earlier.

- Put the candle in the slot and cherish your work!

6. Spoon

Tools Required:

- Maple wood

- Waste woodblock

- Lathe

- Roughing gouge

- Wax and Mineral Oil

- Sandpaper

Steps

- Take a piece of the maple with these dimensions: Length: 6 & 1/2 inches, Breadth: 1 & 1/2 inches, Height: 3/4 inch

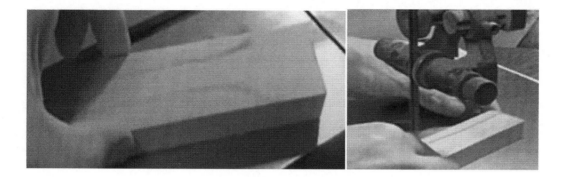

- Mark the handle of the spoon with a pencil, as shown.

- Use a band saw to cut along the marked lines.

- Mark the centers on both ends, as shown below.

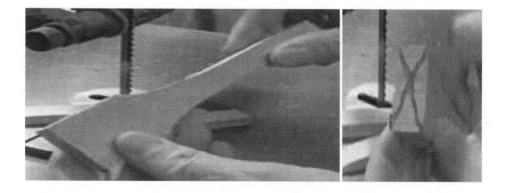

- Put the wood piece in the chuck and start turning.

- Use a spindle gouge to make a concave surface for the spoon head.

- Start on the lathe and use the roughing gouge.

- Turn the wood till you get the desired handle shape.

- Do the sanding using regular sanding paper with grit, depending on the roughness of the wood.

- Use a carving chisel to further shape up the scoop of the spoon.

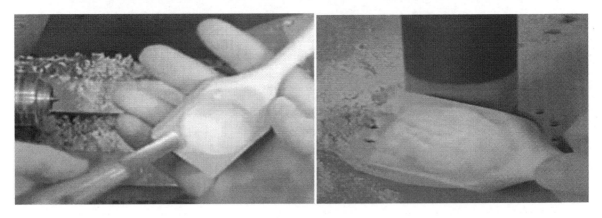

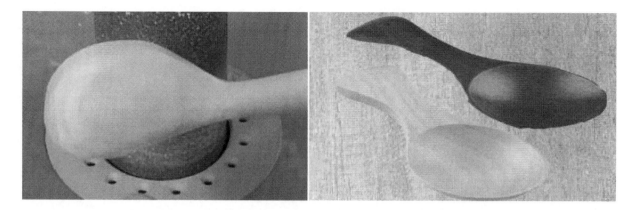

- Lastly, apply food-safe finishing wax and mineral oil of your choice.

7. Ladle

Tools Required:

- Woodblock for scoop and handle

- Lathe

- Roughing gouge

- Wax and Mineral Oil

- Driller

- Sandpaper

Steps

- Take a cubical woodblock for making scoop of the ladle. Draw a circle on the face with a pencil and cut as much as possible before putting on the lathe.

- Run the lathe and use a roughing gouge to shape up the scoop, as shown in the below pictures.

- As the overall shape becomes oval, start with making a concave surface for the scoop, as shown below.

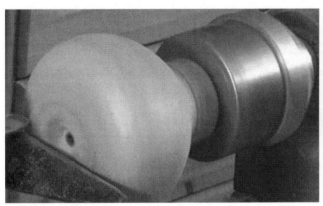 

- Next, move on to make the handle. Put the piece of wood on the lathe and start turning.

- Make a hole in the scoop to fit in the handle. Use glue additionally to strengthen the bond further.

- Apply sanding in both the wood pieces.

- Apply food-safe wax and mineral oil of your choice.

8. Wooden Ring

Tools Required:

- Steel Ring

- Wood plank

- Waste block

- Lathe

- Roughing gouge

- Finishing coating (CA)

- Driller

- Sandpaper

- Rake scraper

- Putty knife

- Glue

- Double-sided tape

- Derlin ring

Steps

- Take a steel ring upon which you would like to have a wooden cover to make a comfort ring.

- Select a suitable plank. It's a critical step. The plank should be a little wider than the ring, completely dried and stabilized. It should not crack up upon working.

- Lay some 120 grit sandpaper on a flat surface and sand one side flat. Once it's flat, apply double-sided tape to the reference face, as shown below.

- Now start turning the wood but mounting it on a waste block using double-sided tape.

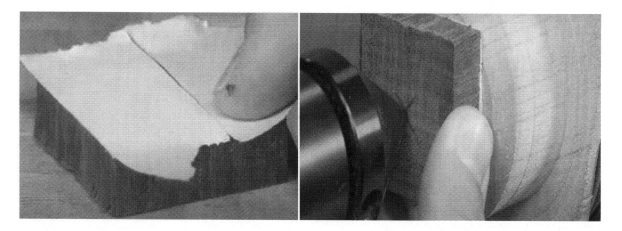

- Peel off the tape backing and line up the center mark with a revolving Center, and with the tailstock in place, rough turn the blank to round.

- Select a drill bit that is approximately half the diameter of the ring core to make a pilot hole. Mount the bit in a drill chuck and drill entirely through the blank, as shown above.

- Using a narrow scraper or skew, laid flat on its side, open up the drilled hole until the ring core fits snugly. Keep testing the ring fitment till it goes inside the wooden hole. Keep 3-4 rings of different sizes as your one ring becomes loosely fitted, you can try the other ones.

- Work on the side of the blank and turn it down until it's just a hair wider than the ring core. Try not to scratch the ring core with the tool. Now carefully peel the blank off the waste block using a putty knife.

- Next, sand the steel ring and glue it up inside the wooden ring. (may use epoxy or CA glue). After gluing the ring inside, swipe away the extra glue outside.

- After the glue is cured, mount the ring between the Delrin ring bushings on a pen mandrel. Start turning it carefully as its delicate.

320

- You can use a negative rake scraper when turning rings because it's not aggressive and easy to control.

- Once it's turned to shape, sand the blank through 320 grit or higher.

- Next, put up a finishing coat, which is shiny (as it is jewelry). You can put 8-10 coats of CA for a shiny surface.

- Enjoy the ring or gift it to a loved one.

9. Turning Tops

Tools Required:

- Spindle Gouge

- Roughing Gouge

- Nose scraper

- Wood plank

- Parting tool

- Lathe

- Roughing gouge

- Finishing coating

- Sandpaper

Steps

- Take up the wood plank and put it on the lathe, as shown below.

- Apply spindle gouge with your fingers running against the tool rest.

- Choose a wood plank large enough for your chuck.

- Use a parting tool to make a tenon.

- Take a sample turning top and make a line at the place with the maximum width of the tabletop. Draw a second line denoting the bottom of the piece. Use a bevel to shape up the handle further.

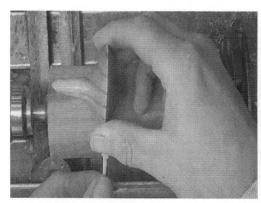 

- After the handle, work on the lower part of the turning top. You have to make it slanted using the bevel and gouge, as shown below. Now use the sandpaper and make it smoother.

- Use denatured alcohol or methylated spirits to clean up and then use Danish oil. Wait for it to dry and then buff it to shine. You can also use shellac.

- The next step is cutting the top from the rest of the wood. Do not use the parting tool bur spindle gouge instead. Apply sanding and finishing to the bottom tip on the recently cut top.

- Now you have your tabletop to play with, enjoy!

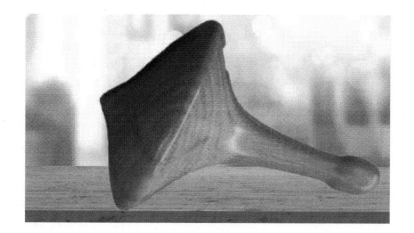

10. Mushroom

Tools Required:

- Spindle Gouge

- Roughing Gouge

- Nose scraper

- Wood plank

- Parting tool

- Lathe

- Roughing gouge

- Finishing coating

- Sandpaper

Steps

- Take a wooden plank and mark centers at the top and bottom face. Now set it into the lathe machine as shown below.

- Use a diamond-tipped parting tool. Now start turning the correct size of tenon as per the set of jaws you have.

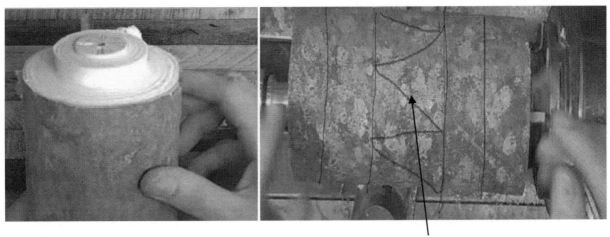

Tenon made as per jaws   Mark the area to be removed

- For rounding off the top, you can use a bowl gouge, spindle gouge, or a skew chisel. The next step is cutting the middle portion, as shown above, as "area to be removed." You can use the bowl gouge again and start eating away at the nub. Now the tailstock may be removed using spindle gouge as shown below.

- Make the center thinner with a realistic bulge at the bottom using spindle gouge. Also, make the roof of the umbrella more natural by undercutting from below (it shouldn't be a flat surface). Also, cut off the base as per the line you have drawn for the base.

- Next, sand it down to 400-600 grit and apply Danish oil as finishing coating.

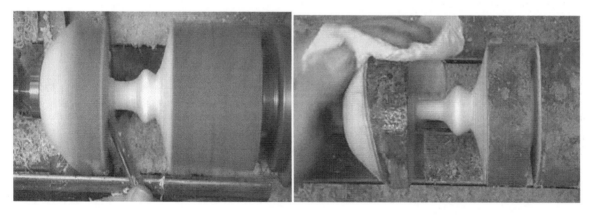

- The last step is to cut off the base of the mushroom from the waste block:

5. Tips, Glossary, and Conclusion

Points to think of if you wish to take woodturning to the next level and start making money. I am throwing a few pointers you can add as per your thought process

- How is your item/project in comparison to your competition in the area you would like to sell in?

- Can you generate sellable quality regularly?

- How long does it take you to produce your products?

- How much do you charge an hour, is it sustainable?

- What are the expenses, and can they be recovered from selling the products?

- Do you have a process and support system in place to produce multiple products?

- Do you wish to make what you want or what the client desires?

- Do you wish to invest 12 hrs a day in the workshop?

- Do you have plans /means to advertise your product in the target market?

- If you are going down the exhibit or gallery path, what's the standard of the display at the gallery?

This is the kind of pastime where people can pick up skills extremely quickly and produce excellent work, yet to take it to the next level needs a lot of business acumen. Do you wish to transform your hobby into a task that you may or may not like going ahead? You are the best person to decide what you want from the craft.

Woodturning Safety and Security Tips

Woodturning is a sub-niche of woodworking, and experienced woodturners can make every little thing from elaborate pieces of furniture to wood clocks, lamps, kids' toys, as well as fashion jewelry boxes and jewelry.

The layout selections are only limited by the skill and the creative imagination of the woodturner.

For professional woodturners and home hobby enthusiasts, woodturning is a rewarding and relaxing pastime; however, much like any other leisure activity involving power tools and sharp devices, there is the risk of severe and even life-threatening injuries.

Though minor scratches are inevitable, following basic woodturning safety and security suggestions can protect against severe injury.

Outfit for Safety

Flying wood chips can create significant injuries to the eyes and face. Wear security goggles that also give side protection.

When needing to work with loud machinery such as a power saw, wear an ear cover.

Pull long hair back from the face, tie it up, and safeguard it under a cap or scarf so it cannot get entangled in the machinery.

Wear fitting clothes, given that baggy clothing, may get stuck.

 No fashion jewelry should be worn, particularly rings, loose-fitting bracelets, or watches. Similarly, never wear a tie while turning.

Bulky tools can fall and damage the feet, so avoid open-toe footwear or shoes and wear safety boots.

Woodturning can send a great deal of dust that can get right up into the lungs and create breathing troubles. Always wear a dust mask when fining sand or turning timber. Some face guards on the market now consist of filters that clean the air efficiently before it is inhaled.

Running the Lathe

Background understanding is essential when you begin turning.

Find a skilled turner and also see the appropriate strategies of running the lathe for different projects.

Check out woodturning publications and instruction video clips, as well as programs.

Thoroughly evaluate user manuals and warnings included with the lathe and all other equipment before using them.

Beginning the lathe at the lowest setting when turning it on, and then get used to the speed needed. As a basic rule of thumb, larger pieces of hardwood require slower speeds, as do unbalanced pieces.

When the lathe has been switched on, it should never be left neglected. If taking a break, turn it off and wait until it comes to a complete stop.

Before trying out a brand-new strategy, practice the move in your mind and then on an item of softwood.

More than normal vibrations, weird smells or noises might indicate that the lathe is not working correctly. Shut off the lathe, and check over the device extensively before returning to use.

Routinely evaluate the problem of the lathe for the right positioning and procedures.

Style of working space

Establish the workspace to produce the optimal environment.

Proper lighting is essential to see clearly while working.

Extension cables can cause electrical shocks and are also a tripping hazard, so it is advisable not to use them.

To give sufficient airflow against dust, it is recommended that a dust removal system be used.

The workshop should also feature windows that can be opened up for airflow and ventilation.

Clean the workspace after each session.

This consists of cleaning all tools and also placing them up out of the reach of youngsters.

Clear the floor and take all equipment off the floor.

Make sure that all the tools are correctly sharpened before starting each project.

Emergency Readiness

Don't panic in case of an accident.

Examine the injury and assess the damage; if the wound needs instant medical attention, call the emergency response number of your location.

Keep a phone in the workshop to obtain fast access to emergency medical services.

To deal with minor cuts and abrasions, maintain an emergency first-aid kit in the workspace.

Always keep a fire extinguisher ready at your workplace and keep it properly maintained.

A running sink in the workstation will be required if dust fragments or chemicals get into the eyes.

In the case of chemical burns, water can likewise be used.

Common Sense Safety Tips

Take notice of your body. Never try to turn if feeling tired out, after drinking, or when heavily medicated.

Keep within the limits of your understanding. Beginners should stay with the processes they understand.

Beginners trying advanced methods by themselves can have alarming repercussions.

Glossary

Woodturning
The craft of using the lathe to generate objects from wood.

Green Timber
Fresh cut logs or timber. They are generally utilized to draft different kinds of projects such as bowls, to permit them to dry completely, and then return to for further work later on. Often used to a final type and enabled to warp creatively. The term refers to damp logs.

Open Form
The lip of the form is continually increasing in diameter in open form vessels.

Closed-Form
In this type of vessel, the lip of the form increases from the bottom decreases eventually towards the top.

Hollow Type
A closed-form with a tiny opening on top.

Pin
A narrow turned piece with the grain ranging from one end to the other.

Lathe
A tool that holds and turns wood while a tool is utilized to shape the wood piece.

Headstock
The part of the lathe that contains the driving mechanism for the lathe.

It is connected to the lathe bed and usually has a spindle for installing faceplates.

Tailstock
An assembly is moving along the bed of the lathe, which can also be secured at any desired placement on the bed.

It consists of a spindle that holds dead centers or live facilities and is typically, however, not solely used in pin switching.

Faceplate
A steel or wood disk installed on the headstock pin and Woodstock is attached to it with screws and holes in the faceplate.

Chuck
Any type of device that holds wood in either jaws or wood is fitted into a cylinder of the chuck.

The chuck is installed on the headstock spindle for working the wood.

Gouge
A device that has a flute and creates a cutting action instead of scraping.

Roughing Gouge
A gouge with fairly thick wall surfaces is used to outline and round stock to a cylindrical shape very quickly.

The edges are not ground back, and the angle around the entire side is about 40 degrees.

By rolling the gouge, you can use the whole side.

Bowl Gouge
A gouge that has a medium to deep flute and is used to rough out and complete the insides of bowls.

Side-Ground Gouge
A gouge that has one or both sides ground back and can be used in a range of placements for harsh, smooth, large scrapes, etc.

Spindle Gouge
A gouge that has a shallow flute and is utilized to generate grains and curves mostly in spindle work (i.e., in between facilities).

Skew Chisel
 Given the name since the cutting edge is at an angle to the tool's side.

The cutting side is usually ground to an angle of 70 degrees.

Parting Device

It is used to make slim recesses or grooves to the desired deepness or to part an item from the lathe.

A typical kind would be the diamond shape, with the center being thicker than the outside to offer the device clearance and avoid friction.

Beading Device

Generally constructed of 3/8th inch square supply and also having angles in 30 degrees and 45 degrees and likewise can be utilized as a parting device.

Scraper

Any type of tool that scratches the timber off rather than cutting or shearing the wood.

A scraper will generally have a very blunt angle and a burr on the edge that does the actual scratching of the wood. It can be likened somewhat to a cabinet scraper.

Chucking

Installing or holding a work surface on some piece of equipment aside from faceplate.

Parting tool

We utilize a parting device to reduce a section of wood to a particular size.

Reverse Chucking

The approach of turning around a form on the lathe to avert the waste near the bottom as well as finish off the piece.

Conclusion

Woodturning in all its kinds is an incredibly popular and pleasurable hobby. The acquisition of good quality lathe, other tools along with a collection of books (online and hardcopy) showcasing and explaining the wood turner's skills will make sure many happy and constructive hours off turning.

Also, we have discussed that safety is of the utmost priority while woodturning. No book or online resource is a substitute for live training, but a supplement to it. Therefore always contact an expert in case of any confusion and follow best practices while woodturning.

This brings to a close the current discussion. It would be very much appreciated if you could leave your feedback on the purchasing platform.

Stephen Fleming

Other Books in DIY Series

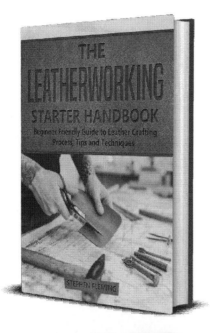

Printed in Great Britain
by Amazon

34260917R00187